Unexpected

How to Be An Amazing Teen Mom

About the Author

Shirley Arthur is a former teen mom. She's the mother of two remarkable young women who have both graduated from college and have successful careers. Shirley graduated from the University of Colorado with a Bachelor's Degree in Business and a Master's Degree in English. She has a successful career in the software industry and lives with her husband in Denver, Colorado and Lahaina, Hawaii.

Also by Shirley M. Arthur

Surviving Teen Pregnancy (Morning Glory Press)

Unexpected

How to Be An Amazing Teen Mom

Shirley M Arthur

Moby Media (Lifestar Publishing)
Denver, Colorado

Copyright ©2014 by Shirley M. Arthur

All rights reserved. This book or any portion thereof may not be reproduced or used in any manner whatsoever without the express written permission of the publisher except for the use of brief quotations in a book review.

Printed in the United States of America

First Printing, 2014

ISBN 10: 0988692503
ISBN 13: 978-0-9886925-0-3
Library of Congress Control Number: 2014916863
Moby Media, Denver, CO

Moby Media (Lifestar Publishing)
3190 S. Ash Street
Denver, Co 80222

www.Moby-Media.com

Preface

Unexpected: How to be an Amazing Teen Mom

I wrote my first book for pregnant teenagers several years ago. It seems that it's time to revisit the issue of teen pregnancy. I now believe that you and your child can not only survive, but thrive. There is a difference. Many people "get by" in life and spend years struggling financially, emotionally, and in their careers. I believe that with the right attitude and mind-set and goals, that your life and your child's life can be successful, happy, and fulfilling.

While the first book was about surviving teen pregnancy (indeed, that was the title), I wanted this book to not only deal with goals and large issues of getting an education, but add more emphasis on emotional and relationships struggles and decisions. This book deals with issues beyond survival.

I still hear "crickets" when I tell people I was a teen mom. I don't always tell people that I was a teen mother, but they can do the math. I tell them sometimes when there is a discussion about how teen mothers are the cause of many societal and financial problems, such as adding a burden to the Medicaid and Social Security systems. The truth is that most teen mothers don't qualify for government aid because they are being helped by parents and grandparents. The truth is that most of the time the financial burden falls on the parents of the teen mother. Most teen parents have to work harder to finish school and to have a successful career. Too many young mothers do not graduate high school. Too many struggle and their children suffer. Being a teen mother isn't easy and it's not something that I recommend to anyone.

I feel I have a responsibility to share what I've learned along the way. Was I the "amazing" teen mother that I would like to say I was? If you look at my children, you might think I was because they are beautiful, successful, and have their own wonderful families, but I made almost every mistake that I talk about in this book.

This book is about rebuilding self-esteem after becoming a teen mom. I don't believe that teen parents should apologize for their children or accept "funny looks" when they walk down the street with their children. We cannot change society as it currently is, but each teen mother can be responsible for her own actions and future.

This book is for all the teen mothers out there who might be struggling to balance their lives between their children and their education. It is for the young women who are afraid they won't have a "real family" or that nobody will really love them and their child. It is for the young mothers who think they don't have the time or the strength or the money to go to college or other vocational training. It is for the young women who feel their relationships with their family and friends has been forever changed or even ruined. It is for the teen mothers who feel they won't be loved when they have someone (their child) who look to them for everything.

Becoming a teen mom is usually unexpected. If you do it right, this unexpected gift can be the best thing that ever happened to you. I read somewhere that almost 50% of pregnancies are unexpected. Being a mother at any age can be a crazy, bumpy, and amazing experience.

one

Unexpected

*"Tell me, what is it you plan to do
with your one wild and precious life?"*
— Mary Oliver, *New and Selected Poems*

It is two months before my 17th birthday. I've always been a sound sleeper and I'm sleeping the deep sleep of someone who needs to recuperate. An insistent noise woke me. I wonder what it is and why it won't stop. Is it the cat crying to get out?

My six brothers and sisters are asleep in various rooms in our rambling, two-story farm house that was built in 1898 in Grand Junction, Colorado. To the East stand the Book Cliffs—foothills of the Rocky Mountains that look like books on a shelf. To the West, I-70 runs straight through Utah, Nevada and California toward the Pacific Ocean. To the North and South lie farms and orchards of peach trees that my sisters and I pick during the fall harvest to make a few bucks. It is cold this February morning, and I don't want to get out of my warm bed.

I should have been thinking about prom and summer vacation and my senior year in high school, but then I remembered. That sound, that crying sound, is my beautiful baby girl hungry for her next meal. She was born the day before Valentine's Day, an unexpected gift from my boyfriend who vanished from my life before I'd told him I was pregnant. Before I'd admitted it to myself.

Once I realized I was pregnant; almost 6 months into my pregnancy, I hadn't had time to get over the denial. It happened too fast, long before I was ready. I wasn't a stupid girl. I'd gotten straight A's through school, was always eager to please, and read books all the time. I rationalized why my period hadn't come: I was irregular; I was upset over "losing" my boyfriend.

Groggily, I stumble out of bed and tip-toe on the cold, creaky wood floors to her cradle. The year was 1968—the height of the Vietnam war, before Roe V. Wade so that mercifully I hadn't had to make a choice, before a time when "keeping your baby" was a choice, and before the now well-known term "teen mom."

The moment I looked into her face after she was born, I felt such natural and intense love. I was naively unaware of the huge job and daily struggles ahead. I was lucky, especially in those days, to have a mother who helped out so much.

My mother was angry for a while. For a long time, in fact, but she was there for me. My father, a quiet and decent man, said, "There's always room for one more at the table."

I decided to keep her because my parents were willing and because a family friend had given me a huge box of soft fluffy baby clothing and blankets. It was a decision a teenager makes before she realizes how very young she is. As unfair as it was to my daughter, I gave only a little thought to how her life would be and how she would be treated and judged. In my adolescent mind, I thought that maybe her father would have a change of heart and be mad that I'd given her away. I thought that she and I would take on the world together. I was right about the second thought.

The nurses repeatedly refuse to bring her to my bed during my five days in the hospital. Each new nurse seems to think that I should "come to my senses" and let her be adopted. On day four, as I long to take her and go home to my parents' house, I walk and stand at the nursery window. A man is standing there looking for his baby—a son, he says proudly. He points to my daughter, not knowing she was mine and says, "Look at that one with the blue eyes and the pretty mouth." He taps on the glass—tap, tap, tap.

"That's my baby," I blurt out with the same naive attitude that got me into this situation. The nurse who's trying to find the man's baby son hears him through the thin glass and scowls at me, takes my daughter's bassinet and moves it all the way to the back, far enough that I can barely see her anymore. The nurse's eyes shoot daggers at me after she does it, just to make sure I know why she did it. The man looks at me and shrugs, quickly distracted by his own

baby son, who has now been moved to the front. I see the understanding flash across his face. I'm not married. I'm one of "those girls." I've become adept at reading expressions. His is one of pity and embarrassment. He has unwittingly complimented an unwed mother. At that moment, I feel powerless, hopeless and helpless. I have my daughter and she becomes my joy for the coming years while I struggle to get through school and "make something of myself."

On some level I believe that my daughter remembers that event, being taken from her spot in the front and shoved to the back, out of sight, because someone admired her before they knew she had a shy, once religious, once A-student pariah for a mother.

I believe that was the beginning of my daughter's fight and determination to be seen and heard. And, she has made her mark on the world in big and important ways.

I also believe it was the first of a long string of incidents that led to my self-determination to make something of myself, to graduate from college, to send my own children to college, to be respected and heard.

Times have changed, but other things remain the same. Many young women have long since walked through the fire of raising a child under difficult circumstances.

Those of us who have walked through that fire should be there for you. Every year a million women nineteen and under get pregnant in the United States. It's an astonishing number, considering the availability of birth control and access to information. The Center for Disease Control estimates that between 400,000 and 600,000 U.S. teen moms decide to keep and raise their children every year. How do you undertake this monumental task of being responsible for raising another human being while keeping your own goals, taking care of yourself?

Life sometimes brings unexpected gifts and challenges to us, and sometimes they are wrapped in the same package.

Vision

"I find television very educating. Every time somebody turns on the set, I go into the other room and read a book."
— *Groucho Marx*

I love television. I see it as a view of the world as others see it (for good or bad). As I write this, the *Teen Mom* and *16 and Pregnant* series are popular. I watch every one of the stories and get caught up in their lives. It is reality, and yet it's changed by the fact that the girls get paid to be on the show. That's the thing about "reality." Small things change the course of lives, and money and help are two of those things. Most of the "reality moms" end up driving nice cars and getting their own apartments by the end of the series. I don't think it's a bad thing; it's a way for them to earn money while opening up their lives. But is it real?

It shows me that while things have changed for teen mothers, many of the emotional, financial, and relationship struggles remain the same.

Why are there so many unexpected pregnancies among teens? Is it because teens are simply more sexually active now at earlier ages? We have many more birth control choices now. Are teens too young to understand the need for birth control? I don't think so. I think much of the reason for early pregnancy is simply the relaxed attitude of teens about sex. Most teens know the risks of pregnancy and disease that come with sex, but they don't think it will happen to them. They don't consistently use protection. Teenagers consistently take risks.

Young men expect sex now. Sometimes they threaten to move onto the next girl who will have sex with them. This causes an emotional dilemma for young women who are driven to find love and acceptance. Girls, more than boys, are driven by emotion and by a yearning for love and connection to a young man. Many teens are a little naive about their ability to become pregnant, so they take risks. Or, they romanticize pregnancy and purposely become pregnant in order to hold onto their guy. Guys are reluctant (still!) to buy condoms, or don't want to spend the money, or don't believe the girl will get pregnant. There are hundreds of reasons why teen pregnancy happens. But, it only takes one night of unprotected sex to get pregnant.

While Abortion is legal and available, abortion is not an option for every young woman. With much of the stigma of being a young mom removed, more young women choose to keep and raise their babies. There is more public comment and discussion about abortion. Some girls wait too long for abortion to be a choice. Fewer young pregnant women get married or end up with the baby's father. Many times the couple intends to stay together, but the stress of caring and supporting a child tears young couples apart. That means that more young women and their families need help with parenting.

No one choice is easy and pregnancy changes any woman's life forever. In spite of open adoptions and the real and desperate need for adoptable babies, most teenagers who give birth choose to keep and raise their children. It is estimated that only 2% of young women choose adoption. This is the opposite of when I was a young mom. There may be differences in minority births and the availability of adoptive homes. For any mother, it is just plain hard to place a baby for adoption. It takes a certain young woman, a certain set of circumstances, a certain set of adoptive parents, and a good support system to pull this off.

There is a period of time, say the first six months or so of a child's life, during which it might still be possible to place the baby for adoption without too much trauma to the child. This option is sometimes a good one for young mothers who figure out how hard it is to care for a baby while still maturing themselves, or for young mothers who thought they'd have more support from the baby's father or from their own families. If you need help with this choice, please don't be afraid or ashamed—ask for help from a counselor, teacher, pastor, your parents, or anyone else who might support you with your decision.

Like Alice Down the Rabbit Hole

I wonder if I've been changed in the night? Let me think. Was I the same when I got up this morning? I almost think I can remember feeling a little different. But if I'm not the same, the next question is 'Who in the world am I?' Ah, that's the great puzzle!
Alice from <u>Alice in Wonderland</u> by Lewis Carroll

Regardless of how and why you had a baby and decided to raise it, here you are. Does it seem like you are Alice falling down the rabbit hole? You're running into strange situations and strange people whom you never thought you'd have to deal with. People look at you differently. You might feel paranoid, like people are talking about you and staring at you. It's like the old saying, "Just because you're paranoid doesn't mean they're not after you." People may treat you differently. Friends may fall away or their parents may forbid them to associate with you. You're normal if you feel your world has turned upside down—because it has.

That's what it feels like to be a teen mom sometimes—being dropped from your ordinary teenaged life down a rabbit hole with no real clear direction, few resources, a few friends, and a few clues. Not to mention the exhaustion from caring for a baby twenty-four hours a day. Maybe your parents help you or even provide most of the support, maybe your grandparents babysit, or maybe the baby's father contributes. But, no doubt, the responsibility falls squarely on your shoulders. You're deep into Wonderland, having come too far to turn back and having a seemingly endless road ahead of you. But Wonderland has huge good surprises and rewards both for you and for your baby.

First, congratulate yourself. Maybe there was no baby shower. Maybe not many people congratulated you. Maybe they weren't sure whether to send a congratulations card or a sympathy card (note: we always want the congratulations when a baby is born). Maybe your friends magically disappeared the minute you brought the bundle of joy home. But, you did something incredible, something that many girls have been unable to do—you admitted your pregnancy. You safely had your baby. You accepted your responsibility. How or why you came to this point doesn't really matter. Whether you "made the right choice" or not doesn't matter. What matters is you are a young mother, and you want to be a great mom. You want your child to look back to a happy childhood filled with love and joy. You want to have an amazing life yourself.

Up a Creek

"Onward up many a frightening creek, though your arms may get sore and your sneakers may leak. Oh! The places you'll go!"
–Dr. Seuss, Oh, the Places You'll Go!

Sometimes I really did feel like I was swimming upstream and sometimes even drowning. Sometimes I fleetingly wondered if my family would be better off without me, if there were some way I could disappear… But, what would become of my daughter? That always brought me back.

The first year of having a child is just the beginning, but in some ways it's the hardest. You are physically battered and drained. You may struggle financially. You may argue with your boyfriend or the baby's father. Or, he may simply disappear from your lives like mine did. On top of all the emotional and physical issues, you have a baby who needs you. It sometimes feels like you're a waitress in a 24-hour truck stop without any time off other than a 15 minute break here or there.

What can you do during the first few months to make life easier?

Ask for Help!

> *"Challenges are gifts that force us to search for a new center of gravity. Don't fight them. Just find a different way to stand."*
> *Oprah Winfrey*

Any new parent can become overwhelmed with the tasks of caring for a newborn. Add to that your emotional issues, your physical pain (which you may not have counted on), your fluctuating hormones, and well—it's just plain bad at first. On the bright side, you're young. You can take it. Your body will spring back faster than an older woman. You may be emotionally more resilient because of your youthful attitude, but it is always hard.

The loss of freedom usually surprises many mothers. You cannot take a shower, take a nap, or get lunch without first making sure baby is okay and fed and changed. You may have been told that newborns sleep a lot. True, but not necessarily when you want them to. You need time to get used to the rhythms of the baby's sleep. If you're lucky and organized, your baby will settle into a routine of eating and sleeping at certain times.

The best thing to do at this time is to establish your new routine. Use the Internet, friends, or your parents to help you learn about newborns and how to establish good habits and routines.

The truth is you cannot do this alone. Most likely, you are living with one or both of your parents or another relative. Some of you may have moved in with your boyfriend or his family. You may be surprised that most of the burden of caring for the baby falls on you because you are the mother. If you need more help, ask for it.

Ask for and accept help in a non-confrontational way. Say to your mom, "I know this is hard for you too, but I think I need more help. I feel overwhelmed." If this starts an argument, back away, don't escalate. As you'll discover, parent-child relationships are complicated and even when we're adults and on our own, we can revert to childhood behaviors and feelings as quickly as a light-switch is turned on and off.

If the baby's father is still in the picture, ask him in the same non-confrontational way for help. There are several phrases that might be tempted to slip from your mouth, but you cannot take them back, and they only serve to make your loved ones back away. Some of these are: "you never help me," "you are so lazy," or "I have to do everything myself." It's better to say, "I need help," "I feel so overwhelmed and like I don't have time to do everything," "I'm afraid."

Positive reinforcement works wonders. Thank your mother every day if she helps with the baby. Tell her how tired you were and just needed a night's sleep. Thank your father for holding the baby while you shower or take a break. Tell your boyfriend that you feel lucky that he's sticking with you, and with his help you can do this together.

My Life is Out of Control

It's common to feel that your life has spun out of control. You don't have time to take a shower or a nap or catch up on how your friends are doing. Even with help, you have a full-time, non-paying job; your boss is younger than you and he or she is a real baby... Remember that this is temporary, even if it seems like it will go on forever. Your baby will eventually grow more independent with your help, but for now, a schedule helps.

Write a schedule of what you need to do each day. (This shouldn't take more than a few minutes). Put everything on your schedule, including bathing the baby, taking a shower, doing laundry, making plans to go back to school. Once you've written your schedule, go over it with someone like your mother or grandmother or sister. Ask for help if you need it. Tell them you feel overwhelmed and listen if they say they are overwhelmed too. Making this schedule shouldn't make you more anxious, but should help you put things in priority. Are there things that you can cross off? Some of the things that you did before the baby came along may have to go (like getting nails done or spending a lot of time on your hair). This doesn't mean you need to neglect yourself—that will make things worse, but you need to see where you can steal time to do the things you need or want to do.

You also need to plan for the unexpected. Babies get sick and need more attention. Maybe your car broke down and you need to take time to have it fixed. Everyone has these unexpected events, but if you expect them, they won't push you over the edge when they happen.

So…

Don't change anything but diapers right now. Resist the urge to make drastic changes–moving out of your parent's home, leaving the baby with someone just for a while, or getting a new boyfriend. If you or your baby are in danger or are being abused physically or emotionally abused, or if you are kicked out of home, then you need to change where you live. Then you need to find help. Take advantage of what you have now. Sometimes stability is a good thing. It's easy and dangerous to make huge life decisions while we're already under extreme stress. It may not be your dream life to live with your parents and a baby. You may feel caught between two different lives. It's easy to compound mistakes and to send your life spiraling downward. There's no reason it cannot spiral up, it's just that it takes time. If you're in a reasonable living situation, do what you can to make it work. If there is drama or border-line abuse in your house, try to de-escalate and discuss.

Your new life might have been unexpected, but you can have a great life and create a great life for your child.

Tools for Your Journey

Here are some things that might help besides just putting one foot in front of the other, doing what you need to do, and trying to stay positive. First you need to survive the first 30 days. It takes 21 days to form a habit. Toward the end of the first 30 days it will get easier. Then you can start to figure out how to reenter your public life. After that you can start to figure out how to not only survive but also *thrive!*

- **To Do List:** Make a list of things you need to do every day, every week, and so on... Add to it until you have a solid plan for each day and week.
- **Share your list**: Go over this with your parents or grandparents if they are helping you.
- **Ask for help**: If you get turned down, go somewhere else for help.
- **Thank you:** Remember to thank your "helpers." A simple "thank you" or "I appreciate what you're doing for me" goes a long way in soothing a difficult situation.
- **Keep connected:** Connect with other young moms. Every community has a young mom or teen mom program or high school.
- **Don't make any huge changes right away:** Stress adds up. If you don't have to move right away, then don't. If you don't have to decide to break up with your boyfriend right away, then don't.
- **Stay Positive:** Minimize negative people and situations in your life. Have a gratitude list. Be thankful for those good things you have and the good things that will come into your life and your child's life.

two

The Journey Begins

It's my first day back at high school after having my beautiful baby daughter I miss her and I feel fat. I'm surprised that I no longer fit into my jeans and my "jelly belly" hasn't gone away after two months Guarded looks and whispered comments seem to be the order of the day. Everyone keeps a safe distance except for my friend Chelsea who was genuinely excited to see me and acted like nothing had happened. Someone leaves a condom in my locker. When I open the door it falls to the floor, floating and drifting like a paper airplane to the floor. Several kids look at it, then at me. I don't know how they got my locker combination. Could it have been a teacher? I'm called into the principal's office and he reminds me that I'm being watched closely. I don't say anything about how I'm being looked at or about the condom in my locker. He continues talking without asking me how I'm doing. He tells me that anything I do "wrong" and I'm out. He looks hopeful that will happen. I go back to class. My geography teacher, the same one who gave me an A+ at the beginning of the year, gasps when she sees me and leaves the room. I realize that she wanted the principal to ban me from her class. She comes back ten minutes later and never looks me in the eyes again. My former "boyfriend" travels with a group of friends and they float past me now and again, unseeing, as if I'm a ghost.

I'm determined. I don't know what else to do but soldier on. I make it through one year and three months of high school. I graduate with my class. I don't have the A average that I wanted and I totally screw up the SATs, but I make it.

I soon realized that people didn't embrace my child as openly as my family had. It wasn't her fault—she was beautiful and smart beyond her years. It was my fault. I was a teen mom, or an "unwed mother" as we were called back-in-the day. I was a little naive (make that a LOT naive) about people's intentions and feelings toward me. Boys seemed interested in me probably because they thought I'd be an easy mark. Girls avoided me at the urging of their parents who thought pregnancy by association wouldn't be the best choice for their daughters. Teachers put me at the back of the class. I later found out that most of them were in favor of banning me from coming back to school at all. One counselor told me that they had decided to let me come back as a "lesson to others."

Bristol Palin, in a television interview, talked about how it isn't "fun" being a single parent. It may have been the understatement of the year, but the fact is that much about being a single parent is—well—solitary. You may have you parents, or siblings, or a friend may stop by once in a while, but you may find that they don't stay long. They may be afraid of being sucked into the endless abyss of work that you've seemingly cut out for yourself, or they may not know how to help. They may be afraid you'll ask them to babysit or that you'll ask them to help with money. Your boyfriend, if he's still in the picture, may have the same fears. A baby is a huge responsibility. You may find that it's hard to find a babysitter, that they cost money, that your mother or sister may not want to babysit all the time for you. You'll find that babies cost money—and lots of it. They need diapers and formula (if you're not breastfeeding) and they seem to outgrow their clothing every week.

My mother, as generous and wonderful as she was when I was a teen, got as frustrated and fearful as any mother does when her child becomes pregnant too early. She used to say things like, "You're up a creek without a paddle," and "You made your bed now lie in it."

No Self Pity

I never saw a wild thing
sorry for itself.
A small bird will drop frozen dead from a bough
without ever having felt sorry for itself.
<u>Self Pity</u> *by D.H. Lawrence*

I'm not so sure D.H. was right—I've seen plenty of birds that look pitiful and sad when it's freezing outside my Denver, Colorado home. Sometimes the sight of them causes me to get out the birdfeeder and fill it with seed.

Something I do know is that there are a few emotions that cause our forward progress to stall.

Humans are emotional beings. We have the ability to reason, but sometimes this ability causes us to trip ourselves up. We have the ability to think which sometimes gets us into trouble. Some emotions, if we stew in them for too long, can cause a downward spiral into despair and depression. For me, these emotions are **self-pity, envy, jealousy, and self-doubt**. Other people struggle with anger and depression. We have many unanswered questions; some of which we know the answer to but need to ask anyway. *Why did this happen to me? Why do other girls have unprotected sex all the time and never get pregnant? Why do some guys stay and some guys leave? What did I do wrong?*

Envy and jealousy are close in nature, but a little different in that we feel envy when someone else has something that we want. Jealousy arises from suspicion for the large part, or evidence that someone might be winning or someone or something that we wanted. Jealousy to me is much more negative and destructive than envy. Envy can sometimes cause us to work toward what we desire, such as a college education or a great job or house. Jealousy causes people to do crazy things like fight a romantic partner, or destroy someone's personal belongings.

Sometimes emotions are not an enemy, but our subconscious trying to tell us something. I remember an Oprah show about fear and trusting your feelings of fear.

For instance, you enter an elevator with a man and you're fearful. He gets off the elevator on the same floor that you do. You're even more fearful. What Oprah's guest suggested was at that point, get away. Go to another floor. Stop on a floor where there are lots of people. Trust your intuition.

It's hard to tell when to trust an emotion and when to slow it down or snuff it out. It might help to find someone to talk about it logically. It should be someone who is not emotionally invested in you or your future. Maybe it's a teacher or a friend who you trust completely. I'd suggest a parent, but your mother may have the same fears and suspicions you do. You know your mother or grandmother and how they have reacted to your pregnancy. If she is negative constantly or makes you feel bad about yourself, then she isn't the right person to trust all your emotions to.

I believe that if you're overcome with jealousy over one person in particular, that there might be more to the emotion. If you're jealous of a girl that your boyfriend is becoming close to or talking a lot about, are you jealous because he really is getting close to her? Sometimes our emotions are our instincts trying to tell us something. It's important to examine these feelings. Do you know deep down inside that he might be cheating? If so, talk to him about these feelings in a neutral setting, away from the baby, and possibly with someone else in the room, such as a counselor.

Self-pity though goes hand-in-hand with self-doubt. We all feel sorry for ourselves at times. Too much self-pity can cause inaction and what you need when you've got a child is *action*. You need to move forward. What do you do about self-pity? Recognize when you're feeling sorry for yourself and how you're talking to yourself. A lot has been written about negative self- talk, such as "I'm such a loser," or "I just can't catch a break." I talk more about self-talk and expectations in a later chapter, but for now, just know that if you catch yourself in a cycle of negative self-talk, force yourself to say something positive about yourself or your life.

Give yourself a few minutes each day to analyze your feelings. Your feelings matter because they color your choices, they drive your future. If you're feeling sorry for yourself, allow yourself five minutes or so a day for a "pity party" or to cry. If you're angry, try to empty your mind. Remind yourself not to dwell on those things that made you angry; something someone said, something someone in your past did, or something your boyfriend didn't do. Don't give negative emotions any more time than they deserve. Don't dwell too long in the land of the past or in "what ifs" and "I should have dones." What matters is how you handle yourself NOW and in the FUTURE. What matters are the memories you make for your child each day and what kind of future you make for the two of you.

I Don't Feel Like Going Back to School

"I believe that anyone can conquer fear by doing the things he fears to do."
Eleanor Roosevelt

I'm sitting in the auditorium with my graduating class. I'm happy and relieved to have made it. My parents are in the audience. I am afraid when they call my name to get my diploma, but I hear only applause and cheers.

I remember feeling dread at the thought of going back to high school. The experience wasn't without drama and trauma, especially considering how it was back-in-the-day... It wasn't easy to concentrate or even stay awake at times, and it certainly wasn't easy overhearing taunts and rude remarks from fellow students, but I survived and the experience gave me the courage to go to college.

Go back as soon as you are physically able. Don't put it off. The longer you put it off, the harder it becomes. Find a capable adult to provide daycare. If you delay, you may not go back and that can mean huge differences in the way your future and your child's future play out. If you cannot or don't want to go back to traditional school, many towns have alternative schools for young parents or others who do not wish to go to traditional school. GEDs and online study are a good alternative, but in my opinion, it is harder to motivate yourself to self-study, and there is sometimes a feeling that you didn't quite finish high school.

Don't Let Others Define Your Life

You'll get many opinions and much advice from people. Don't take everything to heart. Some people want you to fail to validate their own beliefs about young mothers.

Don't Give Up

It seems like when we are "down" that's the time people least want to help. To me, that's the way things work. Riches seem to flow to the rich and support sometimes seems to flow to those who don't need it. It is a mysterious thing, but something that I think is quite real. If you ask for help and are told no, try again or try another path. There are people and organizations out there willing to help. You have to find the right one, but don't give up. Perseverance and bravery will get you through and someday you'll be in a position to help other people yourself.

Quiet Negative Voices

> *"As a matter of fact, we are none of us above criticism; so let us bear with each other's faults."*
> — *L. Frank Baum, The Marvelous Land of Oz*

You'll likely encounter a lot of advice; scoldings, lectures, and information during your pregnancy and after you bring the baby home. Much of the information is not valid; it is opinion or criticism. Your friends will have opinions, which might range from "it's so cool that you have a baby" to "sorry, I can't hang out with you anymore." Your family will have opinions which range from anger to disappointment to helpful advice. They might continually remind you of what a "fix" you've gotten yourself into.

Advice can be hurtful or it can be helpful. It's important to take any advice you get and not over-think it. If it's something that might help you take care of your baby or make a decision, then certainly think about it and even write it down and go back to it later to see if what you were advised feels right to you.

There is a difference between honest advice that your mother or friend might tell you and a slur or insult. Nobody has to put up with insults and constant bombarding of criticism and name-calling. If you're experiencing this, don't let it build and build until you blow up (something that I did when I was in that situation). The best thing to do is point out to the person that the remark is hurtful and not at all helpful, that you're overwhelmed and a little depressed, and that if they have a positive bit of advice, you're open to it. Don't engage in arguments and escalating insults. They only take away time from your baby and from your healing.

Don't Talk To Yourself That Way

> *To begin to change what's inside you, become more loving toward yourself. In your thoughts, cultivate an inner voice and attitude that's 100 percent on your team*
> —Dr. Wayne Dyer.

Some of the worst dialogue comes from inside of our own skull. We scold ourselves, doubt ourselves, and feel sorry for ourselves. It's part of our nature as humans to have emotions and feelings and the power to reason.

Sometimes our reasoning goes astray and can make us depressed or make a difficult situation worse. If you find yourself constantly thinking you are a bad person, or that your life is ruined for good, or that you'll never have a good life for yourself or your baby, then your brain is working overtime to sabotage your forward progress. You will be an amazing mom and some day your child will tell you so. If you find yourself calling yourself names (maybe some of the names others call you), *don't talk to yourself that way.*

I'm Not in Denial

My daughter is about ten months old, learning to walk early. I decide to take her to the park with my school books and the two of us sit on the expanse of grass, near the swings and jungle gym. She's an easy and happy and very smart girl. Even though she's easy, I can hardly concentrate on my studying. I'd left it for the last minute. My daughter totters and laughs and plays innocently across the grass. I feel happy. Then, I feel a little guilty for feeling happy. I'm not sure why.

A man approaches us. He is older, maybe thirty.

Before I know it the man is sitting beside me and points to my daughter. "She can't be yours," he says. It isn't a question, more of a statement of fact.

"Yes," I said. He proceeds to hit on me, ignoring my laughing daughter. He wants to take us somewhere fun. I quickly grab my things and my daughter and we walk back to my house—which is quite a distance. Why had he assumed she wasn't mine? And why had he looked at me strangely when I admitted she was

mine? For a split second, I had some kind of experience where I didn't know what was true and what wasn't.

Denial is a mysterious and dangerous thing. Denial causes some women to completely reject the idea that they are pregnant or that they are old enough to be a responsible mother. When we hear or read about a young girl who gives birth alone and abandons the baby, we thing, "what kind of monster could do that?" *What kind of idiot would not know she was pregnant? She must have known.* Denial does this. Denial is our mind's way of letting us deal with something that is too enormous for us to grasp.

Denial doesn't stop with pregnancy sometimes. After giving birth, a woman can have a tough time grasping that she's a mother and that the baby is a person who needs her. Sometimes denial leads to depression, either "baby blues" or more dangers post-partum depression.

Along with denial comes "magical thinking."

Magical Thinking

Magical thinking is believing that someone will come along to rescue you. Maybe it will be the baby's father or maybe another man. Even after decades of liberating legislation and women's rights, something in our DNA tells us that a man might come along to take care of us, to love us and our babies as much as we deserve to be loved. Sometimes it happens, but not often.

Or, you might imagine that another adult will take pity on you and give you a job or at least give you a good grade for a class you're taking. I've found that doesn't happen often. Usually, teen moms have to work harder, have to prove themselves even more than ordinary students with teachers, counselors and other adults. If you feel you're treated unfairly, take your case to the teacher and then higher up if you need to.

On the other hand, in most cases people won't give you "extra credit" just because you've got more responsibilities. It doesn't seem fair, but it just *is*. Why is it that people, some of whom are in the business of helping you, seem to go out of their way to make your life harder? I believe it has to do with their sense of judgment about who you are and what you're capable of. Many people who work with drug addicts, for instance, come to believe that most are "hopeless" and most are "not trustworthy." The same with teen mothers. A few teen mothers "go off the rails" and begin partying and some leave their children with relatives. It's your job to prove them wrong. I believe that most teen moms want to be amazing mothers. I believe that most teen mothers can save themselves instead of waiting for rescue.

The opposite of magical thinking and denial is HOPE and HARD WORK.

Do You See a Target On My Back?

It's a year after my daughter was born and I'm at the gynecologist having an exam. I'm nervous of course, and my legs have been put up in the cold steel stirrups, my legs spread wide, and the green cotton cover doesn't quit cover me up. The room is cold and smells of alcohol and antiseptic and danger. There is no nurse in the room, and has never been one in the room during my exams. I feel naked and unprotected. He looks at me when he comes in and comments that I'm young for having had a baby.

He pulls his stool up between my legs and all I can see is his hair. "Do you think you'd like to go skiing with me sometime?" he says

"What?" I ask. I feel like I've been violated in some way, even though it is long before the days when women talk about being sexually harassed. I stare at the slick colored picture on the wall of a uterus and ovaries and at the glass bottles of cotton balls and syringes with their chrome tops.

"I'll think about it," I said, although I'd already thought about it all I wanted to. I wanted to get up and run.

I felt sometimes that having a baby at a young age made me more of a target. Men seemed to think that I was "fair game" or "easy prey" as they say. I felt naked and unprotected. I skipped my gyno appointments for years until (finally), women doctors started miraculously graduating from medical school.

I read somewhere recently that men were going to shopping malls and large discount stores "shopping" for young single moms. Maybe they're pedophiles and maybe they aren't. The point is to have your radar on, to make people earn your trust, and don't assume that everyone (or anyone) wants to help you or make your life better.

You'll get advice from many people, including your friends, your parents, your teachers, and even doctors. MY advice about advice is to take what is useful to you and ignore the rest. Give it good consideration, but make a decision about whether it is advice or criticism or just plain abuse.

Desire to Regress

Some young moms seem to regress into behaviors that seem immature to others. They want others to take care of them, perhaps the same way they were taken care of as children. Maybe your mother is willing to do this, or your grandmother, but it's better to recognize that you're doing it. Your baby needs his or her mother.

If you make yourself "irresponsible" or not capable of taking care of your baby, then you won't have to. Right? Could be, but the long-term outcome could be losing your child or damaging his childhood.

Now is the time to "act as if" you know what you're doing and except help. Don't turn over all responsibility to someone else.

If you think you're regressing or reverting to childhood behavior, try to talk with an adult about it and about how to change your behavior. Maybe your mother or grandmother is getting irritated with you about it. At a calm moment, sit down with her and discuss how frustrated you're feeling and about how you don't really want to act that way.

Desire to Retreat

Almost as bad as acting out and wanting to go out partying every night is retreating. If you're an introvert anyway, it might seem safe and normal for you to stay home all the time, to avoid people, to cocoon yourself into a safe place. Maybe you feel you should be punished. Staying home all the time isn't all bad as long as you're taking care of your baby, but it can lead to phobias, including agoraphobia (fear of open spaces or of leaving your house). Retreating can lead to depression, including the most dangerous kind of post-partum depression. Retreating can prevent you from moving your life forward, from going to school to get your diploma, from going to college, from meeting new friends, and from getting a job.

Another way of retreating, especially these days, is with alcohol or drugs. Drugs seem to be easier to come by and may seem to calm you or make your life easier. They may be prescribed or not, but one thing for certain is that all drugs have side-effects. If you find yourself retreating, try to do one thing every day that gets you and your baby out of the house, even if it is going to the store or the library or the shopping center to walk around. Sometimes a walk each day helps or taking the baby to a play group so you can talk with other parents. There are online groups now for all types of mothers, including teen moms.

So…

Are your fun days over? Not by a long shot. You have a lot of life ahead, and that means fun times along with work. You can still have friends and go out with them when you have a reliable babysitter. You can responsibly date and make new friends. You don't need to rush to find a boyfriend or to get married. You can do fun things with your child. A bonus of having your children young is that you'll be young when they are grown. You'll be able to enjoy grandchildren at a younger age. You'll be able to have more freedom in your forties and fifties than most people. That may not seem like an advantage now, but you will see it as your child grows and gets more independent. If you do a good parenting job, your child will grow into a responsible loving son or daughter.

So many opportunities await you. You can be a doctor or a lawyer if you want it badly enough. You can own your own business or be an inventor. You can be a chef or open a restaurant.

Tools for Your Journey

- **Activities:** Make a list of activities you want to do with your baby.
- **Keep a Journal:** It helps to write down your feelings and reread to know your success or things you need to work on.
- **Thank You:** Continue to thank your "helpers." A simple "thank you" or "I appreciate what you're doing for me" goes a long way in soothing a difficult situation.
- **Ask for Help.**
- **Connection:** Connect with other young moms. Every community has a young mom or teen mom program or high school. Even an online blog for young moms or a social media site can help. Don't rush relationships with new guys.
- **Gratitude:** Minimize negative people and situations in your life. Have a gratitude list. Be thankful for those good things you have and the good things that will come into your life and your child's life.
- **Self-Talk:** Keep your self-talk positive. Don't say anything to yourself that you wouldn't say to your best friend.
- **Regression and Retreating**: If you think you're doing this, talk to someone about it.
- **Watch for Denial**: Do others tell you that you are in denial about your situation? Do you feel a sense of unreality or confusion? These are things to talk with a counselor or trusted adult about.
- **Snuff negative thoughts:** try to recognize if you are spending too much time with negative emotions such as envy and jealousy, or anger. Measure your mood levels. Are you depressed?

three
Incredible Disappearing Friends

Here's what happens:

You get pregnant. You're shocked, in denial, scared, and worried. You perhaps tell the baby's daddy. You might tell your best friend before you tell your parents. Or, you might tell your sister. Then, if you find it hard to tell your mom and/or dad, you put it off until you're showing or even a little longer. One or two friends might know, but it's your secret. When you finally tell your parents, all hell breaks loose. It's a lot for them to handle, and there's a lot of drama.

Some of your friends might disappear at this point, maybe because they cannot take the drama or don't want to be associated with a girl who is pregnant, or for a variety of other reasons. Maybe one or two of your friends stick by you. Then, you have the baby. Your entire daily life changes and melds into 24 hours of crying wriggling baby, with or without help from your family. Your friends might drop by to see the bundle-of-joy, but one by one, they drop out of your life.

Why does this happen? It isn't really because your friends were bad people or even that they are disloyal. It's that *your* life has changed. *You* have changed. You're a mother now, and not every young girl can handle the immense amount of work and constant care and attention a newborn requires. You're probably having trouble with it yourself. Your boyfriend or baby-daddy might be having trouble with it. You can't go out whenever you want, and if you do, it has to be to a baby-friendly place. If you're being a good mom, you're not partying as you did before you became pregnant.

It might not be fair, but it's a normal progression of events that nobody tells you when you're pregnant.

Can You Maintain Your Former Life?

If your life-before-baby was a lot of partying and socializing, then probably not. If you go out more than once a week (I'm talking about going out "partying") then you're probably not taking adequate care of your baby, or your mother or other relative has the baby much of the time. It's almost impossible to keep the same style and level of social life you had before your pregnancy, unless of course, you're one of those people who stays home and studies. If you leave your baby with your parent or relative, it probably should be to go to school or work–the things that are going to change your life. You do need a break now and then. You need to get out with or without the baby to do things so that you don't become depressed. These are things you need to work out with your family and friends.

As your life changes course, so will your friendships and relationships. Watching your friends leave, become cold or distant is emotionally upsetting. Isolation can lead to despair and loneliness. Trying to keep up with former friends can lead to strained relationships with your child and your family. How can you build new friends and a healthy network of people who support you?

Find New Friends

If your friends start falling away, don't fight too hard against it. They are probably on a different path than you. It's better to meet new people and make new friends than to try to keep up with your old ones. I think many young moms get caught up in trying to act like their single friends, and it just doesn't work when you're a mother and when you're trying to finish school and earn a living for you and your child. Join a single mom group. Even finding an online group or forum can be helpful.

Don't try to hang onto current friends if they are not accepting of your baby. You don't have to have a big "break-up fight" to talk with your friends. Tell them, "Look, I know my life has changed and my baby has to be first priority. It isn't easy for me to go out as often as I used to. If you can still be my friend I'll love you for it. If you can't,

I understand. Or, we can go out every now and again." Believe me, if you phrase it this way to them, they're more likely to stay your friends.

Boys as Friends

Many teen moms look to young men to fill the void left by vanishing friends. Usually this isn't a good idea because, well, you know…

A romantic partner and a friend are two different things, as you know. Young romances are rarely forever, even if you want them to be. Young people need to date several people, sometimes many before they find the right person. This makes friendship difficult. I'm not saying you can't have male friends; you certainly can, especially if they are part of a group of friends. However, trying to find a guy to take care of you or be with you cannot take the place of female friends.

There are some young men out there who can really be a friend to you, but usually they are just looking for sex. It's not usually a good idea to get emotionally hooked on another guy. Most likely it won't last because most young relationships don't. You're exposing your child to one or many men coming in and out of their life. You're opening yourself up for more hurt or rejection.

Many young teens that appear on MTV's *Teen Mom* series seem to be desperate to either hang onto the guy they have or to find someone else. Usually they say they don't want to be "alone." This is ironic because when we have children, we are never alone. What young moms usually mean is that they need adult companionship that cannot be filled by a baby (or a mother who might be slightly angry with you).

When you're young you have a lot of time. Logically that time should be spent with your child and getting an education. I know (having been there) that much of your time is spent wondering if you're going to be alone, or figuring out how to "redeem yourself" with another guy or with the baby's daddy. The reasons for this drive to bond with a male partner are hormones and chemicals in women's brains that become more intense during and after a pregnancy. These hormones drive us to want to nest with someone. Just understanding this might help you understand why you feel desperate for "a man to love you and take care of you."

Sometimes it's easier to find another boyfriend than it is a girlfriend. That doesn't mean you should quit trying. Just focus more on friendships than a girl-guy relationship for now.

Find Other Young Moms in Your Area

Your school might have a teen mom program. If not, there are support groups in every town. You can research these or ask a counselor or even try Planned Parenthood. A support group can become a source of lifetime friends. You can help each other, share clothing and baby items, and even trade babysitting services.

If you cannot find a support group in your area, consider starting one. The act of doing this can help you feel empowered as well as help you make friends and help other. It might seem time-consuming, but it's something that you can do and take your baby along.

Forums and Chat Groups

The Internet can be a good place for growing a support system. You can use online forums (find a reputable one) and online chats to discuss issues and problems with other young moms. It's something you can do when baby is asleep or when you've got a few minutes break. Don't let it become too obsessive and it can be a good source of information and comfort. Watch for stalkers and don't pay attention to rude comments.

Are You Shutting Others Out?

On MTV's *Teen Mom* show, a girl named Farrah, couldn't seem to let any other girls in as friends. She constantly bemoaned the fact that she was alone, seemed to constantly cry, seemed on a desperate hunt for a new boyfriend, and sometimes seemed to neglect her child and blow up at her parents (who were trying to help her).

Does this sound like you? Farrah seemed to shut others out, even those people who tried to help her. She withdrew from her friends (or they withdrew from her) and this hurt her so much she was afraid to make new ones.

Just understanding this fear of making and losing friends, and the feelings of rejection that come with it, can help you move forward with making new friends. People come and go during a lifetime. Some friendships stick and others do not.

So…

Pregnancy and birth have changed you. It's inevitable. When we change, our relationships change. Hold onto the fact that this change can be a good one and that you can control how your life goes and who comes into and out of it.

Tools for Your Journey

- **Join or start a teen mom group.**
- **Make new friends at work or school.**
- **Confide, don't hide.** If you feel isolated or lonely, reach out to family members, a trusted counselor, or support group.
- **Keep writing in your journal.**
- **Remember to review your goals.**
- **Take your baby with you:** You can get out of the house AND have the baby with you. Most cities have baby-friendly and often free activities. Check online.

four
Your Family; Do they The Hate You?

My baby has been born and most of the dust has settled around the sand storm that I'd caused earlier in the year. It's June and my baby was born in February. I've finally gotten enough nerve to attend a family event; a dinner at my aunt's house with my three cousins and my grandparents. I'm in the kitchen helping my aunt with the dishes. Usually warm and chatty, my aunt angrily picks up plates, washes them, and hands them to me to dry. I continue drying the dishes and wondering if I should just leave. Usually quiet, I start chattering about something to fill the cold silence—going back to school or something about my baby. I can almost peel the ice off the space between us. I can't wait to take my baby and go home. I'm puzzled why she'd allowed me to come to dinner if she hated me. Maybe my parents hadn't asked her if I was welcome. I'm sure she hates me. I'm sure my grandparents hate me. I'm pretty sure my immediate family just tolerates me.

Bristol Palin is the daughter of famous politician and speaker, Sarah Palin. Her mother was a conservative Republican when her daughter Bristol told her that she was pregnant with her then boyfriend's child. Bristol Palin said in an interview that telling her mother she was pregnant was "harder than labor."

It was so hard that she didn't break the news herself, but instead brought along a friend who blurted out the news . Now *that's* hard. But, she's right. Telling your family you are pregnant IS emotionally harder than labor in some instances. Some girls have always been able to talk to their mothers about sex and birth control, but even they sometimes say that it was hard to tell their mother about their pregnancy. Why? None of us want to disappoint our parents or our families.

Most of us want them to be proud of us, no matter how strained our relationships. For some girls it's harder to tell a parent who has been open about birth control and sex. Who wants to tell her mother about a surprise pregnancy after years of sex talks and open discussion?

Some girls never work up the courage and have their babies on their own, or they run away, or their family finds out when they are rushed to the emergency room. Sadly, some young women never tell anyone; they give birth alone under dangerous circumstances. There are no valid statistics as to how often this happens because there could be instances where nobody finds out.

The urge to please our parents is strong. The thought of disappointing them or making them angry and reject us is powerful. So, if you've already told your family (which I suspect you have if you are reading this book), then congratulations. You've made it over a huge hurdle. If you haven't, I can only say that there isn't an easy way. Don't hide your pregnancy. Tell someone, even if that someone isn't your parent or family member. Don't hide, confide.

Cautionary Tales

Sometimes my husband accuses me (rightly) of always reading the negative stories. I do this. I'm attracted to train wrecks. I think many women are (and a few men). I choose to believe that I read these stories as "cautionary tales" or stories designed to make me avoid making terrible mistakes.

There are a few stories I should give up, such as celebrity break-up rumor stories and stories that may or may not be made up about mice in our fast food and people who won the lottery and were broke in two years. Some stories truly have a message though. I read teen parenting and teen pregnancy stories and watch the "pregnant teen" shows on television. I look at them from a slightly different perspective though, as someone who has been there. In some ways these show do harm to pregnant teens and single mothers. The problem with the shows is that in the first season the mothers are shown more realistically. The young couples on these shows are mostly broke and scared. They struggle.

They are somewhat lost and needy. By the second season, after they've been paid by the network, they turn up with cars and hair extensions and new apartments. The truth is many young single mothers and young couples struggle every day to maintain jobs and school and a place to live.

Then there are the extreme tragic stories. Two news stories stick in my brain because they were so tragic and so predictable on hindsight.

You might recall the story of Casey and Caley Anthony from the news. Casey Anthony was nineteen when her daughter was born. Despite being almost safely out of her teens when she became pregnant, Casey seemed to behave more like a young teenager during her pregnancy and after. Casey didn't tell her parents or anyone she was pregnant until she was almost eight months along. When she did, her parents took control, mostly her mother, as she usually did. They insisted that Casey keep the girl and let them "help" her raise Caley.

It seems that a dysfunctional family existed before Caley's arrival, and it only got worse after Casey began going out with her friends again to party, lying to her parents, and stealing from them and her friends. Things escalated between Casey and her mother, and eventually Casey took her young daughter and moved out of the house.

Caley Anthony was found murdered and dumped in a swamp not far from Casey Anthony's home. What happened? We won't ever really know unless Casey tells us more, but, wanting to go out at night, did she begin sedating her child to make her sleep? Was she a cold-blooded killer, or was she immature and wanted a "night out?" We'll never really know, but we know that she put her child in danger.

Caley Anthony was missing for thirty-one days before Casey Anthony was forced to admit that her daughter was missing. Although Casey went on trial for the murder of her daughter (the prosecution surmised that Casey wanted to party and may have accidently overdosed her daughter and left her in the trunk of her car), she was acquitted and set free in 2011.

While many people blame this tragedy on Casey's mental state and her selfishness, I believe the entire family was to blame. Was her mother extremely critical and controlling as some accused? Was her father over indulgent and angry over Casey's pregnancy? Just the name confusion of having a "Casey" and a "Caley" seems to have some significance. Did

Casey feel replaced by her own daughter? These things are complex and a surprise pregnancy sometimes doesn't give the entire family time to make good decisions and to react in a healthy way.

These tragedies cross racial barriers. While Casey Anthony is white, Shaquan Duley is black.

Shaquan Duley, a single mom of three children, lived with her hyper-critical mother and sister. Possibly suffering from post-partum psychosis, Duley snapped one night when her sister and mother criticized her mothering skills. She drove into a local lake, drowning her two young boys and escaping with her own life. She said she intended to take her own life.

Family members should always be aware of your state of mind. If you are depressed, which you very well might be, or if the depression worsens so that you have thoughts of harming yourself or your child, you need to tell someone. That "someone" might not be a family member if you feel they are part of the problem or that they will minimize your problem.

Call a helpline; tell a friend who is in a position to help; tell a teacher or counselor that you trust to help you and be sympathetic.

How to Deal With Resentment

It might seem like your family resents you. It comes out in many ways: as envy, as anger, as revenge, or as apathy. Angry resentful feeling can escalate to dangerous levels. Resentment can occur within your immediate family, your extended family, and society in general.

In the show MTV's <u>Teen Mom</u> series, young mom Farrah continually faced the alternating love and wrath of her mother. Farrah's mother made it clear to Farrah how disappointed she was. She did this over and over again. We watched Farrah's mother slap her (sometimes after being pushed into it by Farrah), yell at her, tell her how disappointed she was in her, and use her granddaughter as collateral. To make matters worse, many of Farrah's friends deserted her. Further beyond that, because she was a media figure (admittedly by choice); she got blasted on blogs and in the news across the country for "glamourizing teen pregnancy."

Remember that while raising your children, even if you didn't get it from your own parents. I read somewhere that you have two chances to have a good parent-child relationship: the first with your own parents and the second chance with your children. So many families pass down bad habits and relationships and problems and addictions. It doesn't have to be this way.

When you overhear your parents or relatives say negative things about you and your situation, it makes you feel helpless and hopeless. These feelings alone are enough to make a person throw their hands in the air and go party. What if your mother told you at least once a week how proud she was of you for working so hard? What if you overheard her telling your aunt that you are a good mother and student and that you have a bright future ahead? These simple things would raise your expectations and possibly encourage you forward with your goals. And, these things are most likely true. You ARE a good mother. You ARE a good student. You DO have a bright future.

Dealing with friends and with society, I believe, is easier. You should simply look straight ahead toward your goals and achieve them. You don't get angry with them or retreat from them; you ignore them. There is a saying that the best revenge is success. I believe this to be true. Success isn't instant in most cases; it takes years sometimes. It takes persistence and hard work.

What about Siblings?

You didn't intend it, but you've also altered the lives of your brothers and sisters and other members of your family. Maybe they are younger or older, but they've probably taken some heat about your pregnancy at school or work or around the community. This is especially true if you come from a small or tight-knit or conservative community.

You might not have made the choice they wanted you to. Perhaps adoption would have been better for them. They'll be mad at you –maybe for a lifetime.

How can you help your family to heal and help yourself keep a healthy relationship with them? Can you talk with your brothers and sisters and tell them you know how hard it is on them? Can you ask for their help and then tell them how much you appreciate them? In time, most likely, they will grow to love your child and be wonderful aunts and uncles.

You don't intend to live at home forever (if you are), or with other relatives or with the help of relatives. If you live at home with your child, what happens when you move out? It's something I didn't really think about. I thought about how I would feel when I moved out (free and independent), but I failed to factor in how my family would feel and how my child would feel. My daughter was four years old by the time I was independent enough to move out of my family home. When I say "independent" I say it loosely because it took other people to help me do it, and it was after I'd finished two years of college.

Moving away from home was hard on my daughter and it was hard on my family. If I could go back I would probably talk to my family about this. We weren't big talkers back then. Lots of things were swept under the rug in conversation. I think everyone knew that I would move out. Maybe they thought I would leave my daughter there. Had I left my daughter with them, I doubt that would have garnered any more good will than moving out and taking my daughter with me. It's one of those "damned if you do, and damned if you don't" situations, but it's one that you need to discuss with you family. I had never intended to leave my child with my family for an extended period of time. I did leave her with my family for a few summers when she was young, and I am forever thankful to them for opening their arms and hearts to her.

What does your family expect of you in the future? Do they want you to move out and take your child with you, or do they think you'll leave your child with them? What do *you* expect? They might not see you marrying and moving away with your child, but it could happen. They might not see you finishing school and getting a good job. They might not see you staying for an extended period of time in their home, but it might happen.

Family Dynamics

I barely remember what was going on with my brothers and sisters at the time of my pregnancy and during the time I was living at home with my daughter. I appreciated that she had my younger brothers and sisters to play with her and keep her company. It was terribly hard on her when we moved away.

My older sister, just one year older than I, took the brunt of having to deal with my pregnancy. I told her before my parents found out, so she was burdened with that knowledge for a while before I had the courage to let my parents know. I never knew if she was harassed at school about it; we never talked much about it. My parents were angry with her for keeping my secret. I'm sure it didn't help her experience with high school and after. She told me once that it was she, not I, who should have had the first grandchild. I agreed with her, but was powerless to change things at that point.

My older sister and I became farther apart at that point, I believe. I know she didn't want to be appointed "babysitter" or anything like that, as both of us had already had been charged with caring for younger brothers and sisters. My sister married young and had her own children, and it seemed we didn't talk much about her concerns. Again, I was caught up in my own drama and my own problems, and failed to see my sister's point of view. We didn't argue, but I believe there were resentments that we needed to talk about and never did.

Things you can do:

- Apologize to your siblings for disrupting their lives. It's hard to apologize to a brother or sister whom you're used to arguing or sparring with. But, do it. A sincere apology can do wonders. Don't diminish the apology with the "but" word. The "but" word negates an apology. "I'm sorry, but it's not easy for me either." Simply say you're sorry. You needn't say it over and over because then you diminish your own self esteem. Say it once or twice and mean it.
- Thank them for their help for even the smallest things.
- Tell them that you love them and they are great aunts or uncles.
- Ask them what you can do to help them. Do they need to talk? Are they being harassed at work or school? Have they had to defend you to anyone?
- Forgive them for saying mean or ugly things to you. Usually a sibling says something mean out of frustration or even to run away from a tough situation. If they say something ugly to you, de-escalate the situation by telling them you don't think they really mean it. Then, walk away. Never spend energy arguing. It

never helps anything and only causes resentment. Many times resentments last a lifetime.

These emotional things are a lot for you to handle right now during this time that you're struggling with so many other problems. You'll think about it later though, so a little attention to them now will do wonders for your relationship over a lifetime.

Extended Family

Your grandparents, cousins, and aunts and uncles may also have something to say about your pregnancy. If they are helping you (sometimes grandparents step up to help), remember to be grateful for everything they do. Tell them how grateful you are for any kind of help. Ask them if you need help, but ask them to be honest if they can handle babysitting or other kinds of help.

You may be unwanted or unasked for advice from aunts and uncles and cousins. Sometimes there is competition among cousins. It happens if there is competition between your parents and their siblings. It's the "my kids are better than your kids" syndrome. If you feel an aunt or uncle or cousin is gloating about your situation or if you feel uncomfortable in any way around them, simply don't be around them if you can help it. Don't ask for their help and don't leave your child with them.

Sometimes a relative wants you to do things his or her way. For instance, they might want you to relinquish the care of your child to someone else. If this happens, tell them you'll consider it or think about it. Just remember that you are in control of what happens with your child. Don't get into arguments with relatives. It's rarely worth it. If you're being abused or bullied by relatives, that's another story. Tell them you'd rather not talk with them unless you're both at a family event. This might seem like avoidance, but sometimes just staying away from people who are negative or are not good for us is the best policy. If the abuse or bullying escalates, then you can use warnings or legal routes, but this usually isn't needed.

For the most part, extended relatives will warm up to your child and integrate him or her into their lives. If this doesn't happen or if they favor other children in the family and ostracize yours, then the same advice applies; avoid putting yourself and your child in those situations where you or your child are uncomfortable.

Your Parents

They need to address and acknowledge any anger or resentment they have about your pregnancy. You should listen without becoming angry (if possible) or resentful yourself. There is nothing more miserable than not having enough money or time or freedom, as a teen, then becoming even more tied to your parent. The purpose of adolescence is a time to separate from our parents, to become our own selves and make our own lives.

Pregnancy and birth changes all this. Forever. This would be true no matter what choice you made; had you chosen abortion or adoption, the fact is that you became pregnant and your family was probably not (at least in the beginning) happy about that fact.

Your job is to co-exist with your support system as long as you need them; for your sake and for the sake of your baby.

Here are some common scenarios: Mom says she's supportive and to all outsiders, appears to be supportive, but when you're alone she shoots "verbal arrows" at you about how you "made your bed" or "spread your legs" or "you should have thought about that when," etc.

Scenario one—Paranoid Parent

Mom or Dad *say* they support you, but you find them more controlling and stifling than before you were pregnant. They don't trust you and they are angry with you much of the time. They aren't confident that you can be a good parent. They're afraid you'll get pregnant again (or afraid you'll have sex again). They go through your belongings to make sure you don't have birth control or evidence of sex. This is dangerous because if you're sexually active, then you should be on birth control and you should visit a doctor at least once a year. It's doubtful you can change your parents' minds about birth control and abstinence, so keep that in mind when you choose a birth control method.

Some (like IUDs) don't require pill packets and evidence that you're on birth control. So, there are options. There is no need for you to feel like a criminal or a drug addict when using birth control. It's preventative so that you don't get pregnant again.

Scenario Two—Controlling Mom

In the very beginning when you bring the baby home, you're very tired and overwhelmed. Your mom steps in to help or even takes over care of the baby so that you can rest. Maybe Mom never thought you could take care of the baby and has wrestled the responsibility from you. Once this happens and your mother bonds with the baby, it is harder to get control back. You might feel that she thinks you are incompetent. She might even tell you that you're incapable of taking care of the baby. If Mom has taken over and won't let you care for baby or make decisions, you need to sit down and have a heart-to-heart discussion with her. If you don't do it now, you may never gain control over your parenting. It will be harder down the road to leave home and take your baby with you. If this is something you want; if you want your mother to raise your child forever, then you need to make the decision and discuss it with her.

If you want to take responsibility for your child, then you need to make it clear to your mother. You need to step up and do most things for your baby when you're home. Don't make yourself incompetent by drinking or doing drugs or sleeping all day. These actions are a way to remove yourself from responsibility.

Scenario Three—Passive-Aggressive Mom

Mom is passive-aggressive (come here sweetheart so I can slap you, etc). I found with my own mother, she wanted me to feel bad about getting pregnant so young and while single (which I did), and when I showed any sign of joy or happiness, she became verbally abusive when we were alone. I understand now her reasoning; she was adjusting to our new situation and she was trying to make sure I understood the gravity of my situation. She didn't know that I understood it all too well. I was trying to make myself feel better about my situation, and in my usual naive way of doing things, I would make jokes or become happy when the situation didn't warrant it.

When she felt I had slipped down into despair (which for me, was never severe), then and only then could she throw a few words of encouragement at me. I could never have raised my daughter without her and she was a good mother herself, but I had crossed an unacceptable line for the time. This was decades ago, but I wonder if things are much different today for some young women.

If your mother or father seems unable or unwilling to "forgive" you or to accept your situation, then you need to bring it up with them. Instead of retreating and crying, try saying, "Mom, it hurts my feelings when you're mean or when you ignore me or act like you hate me." This might open up a discussion. If it starts and argument, back off and try again later. At some point in the future, all will be forgiven and your mother and the rest of your family will see the good things that came from your early pregnancy.

Validation

I try not to have many regrets and the ones I do revolve around hurting other people. When my oldest daughter was a teenager and I was also young myself, she went through an adolescent period where I thought she "felt sorry for herself." I realize now that I thought I was "toughening up" my two children. I felt that they should be grateful for what we had. We had enough money and a house to live in and food and they were able to have activities and fun. They both had lots of friends and were popular. There were lots of things they didn't have though. They had lived through a divorce and all the emotional stuff that came with it. They didn't have all the latest things other kids had. They worked part-time while going through school.

So, when my oldest expressed sadness or went into the past to dig up old bad memories (and I know her childhood was less than ideal), I was unwilling to talk with her about them. I felt I didn't really listen and not judge and just let her be sad. Sometimes when we hear someone (our child, our parent, our sibling) talk about how sad they were or how they had a rough time with something, our first instinct is to say, "Yes, but what about ME? It wasn't any great picnic for me either."

I was afraid of being blamed for a bad childhood for either of my children. I know now that I was responsible for them and for the experiences they had. So, it *was* my fault, but I can now accept that without kicking myself for it all the time. I know now that everyone needs to have their feelings acknowledged whether *we* think their memories or feelings are correct or not. People remember things in different ways. Two siblings can remember the same event, and one sibling will recall it as traumatic and the other as a learning experience. It's not our place to judge how our loved ones feel about something.

I regret not validating my oldest daughter's feelings and insecurities and regrets over her childhood, which was less than ideal. I know that I alone was responsible for her childhood. I know now that when my daughter was sad that I could have told her that it's okay to be sad. She did have a rough time, and yes, much of it had to do with me and situations that I put her in. I have to live with that, but I can now tell her that I'm sorry about any bad experiences she had. She has a right to be sad and to remember her childhood the way she experienced it. The same goes for my second daughter, who had her own experiences to deal with.

Just saying, "I hear you and I feel bad about it and it's okay to cry," can work miracles. Just saying, "I hear you and I am sorry," can heal an entire relationship.

How to Keep Arguments from Escalating

Power Words

I don't normally believe in magic and I think many young women especially get caught up in "magical thinking" or the "superman syndrome" where we believe someone or some event will come along and save us from our terrible plight. I'm guilty of buying lottery tickets and hoping against hope sometimes, as we all are, but we can do it with a bit of caution.

I do believe some words are "magic" in a way when we deal with those we love. Everyone wants to be heard—not just listened to, but really *heard*. Most children want their parents to be proud of them and most parents want to be appreciated. So, there are some words that are hard to say to children and some words that are hard for children to say. But, once you get them out they can solve an argument or at least deescalate it to a manageable point. They can help you feel loved or help your mother feel appreciated. If you are to the point you don't *want* your mother to feel appreciated or you're not willing to accept love from her or from your dad or from whoever you're having issues with, then it's good to sit down and figure out why. Why can't you tell your mother you appreciate what she's doing for you by babysitting while you're at school? Is it that she calls you a bad mother and it makes you sad? Is it because she criticizes or overlooks everything you do with baby? Is it because she hates your boyfriend?

Writing these things down and really figuring them out will help all of you to sit down and have a fulfilling discussion with the other person and heal your relationship.

Once you figure out your relationship and everyone's hot buttons and insecurities, these words might work magic.

These words will work for your parents and relatives. They will work for you you're your children are older. These are power words:

I love you.
I'm proud of you.
I'm behind you no matter what.
You are a good mom.
You are a good child.
You are (generous, kind, smart, beautiful, etc.)
I'm sorry.
I made a mistake. I know I disappointed you.
I forgive you.

So...

A tremendous power transfer happened when you became a young mother. You became somewhat vulnerable, you have lost a little of your social power, you may have lost some status, and your place in the family. Your family might have more financial and emotional power over you than you wanted. You might be more dependent on them than you ever intended for yourself now that you're a mother.

Remember the power of expectations. Expect much of yourself and of your child. Push yourself. It's hard to be a mom and achieve success, but you can do it. Take it one day at a time, always with your future and your child's mapped out in your mind.

Tools for Your Journey

- **Goals:** Write down your family goals and share them with your family. How long do you expect to live with them? What do you want to happen after you move out?
- **Thank You:** Remember to thank your "helpers." A simple "thank you" or "I appreciate what you're doing for me" goes a long way in soothing a difficult situation.
- **Connection:** Continue to connect with other people. It gets easier.
- **Ask for Help:** Ask your family for help and tell them exactly what you need to make your goals happen.
- **Gratitude:** Thank your family for their help. Let your family members overhear good things you think about them.
- **Take Responsibility:** Try to take care of your baby yourself as much as possible when you are home. Resist the urge to let another family member take over. If you don't know how to do something—learn or ask for help.

Remember You Have Two Chances: You have two chances for a happy and healthy parenting experience; once with your parents and once with your own children.

five

Will You Have the Life You Wanted?

I step off our Nile cruise ship onto a Felucca, a small Egyptian sailboat, for an afternoon sail to a native village at the base of the Aswan Dam. Huge and colorful water birds fly and float by our silk-decorated boat. Tourists on camels line the sand dunes of the great desert only a few hundred yards away. Date palms wave in the breeze. We've just spent five days seeing the major archeological sites in Egypt, from the Great Pyramids to the Valley of the Kings. It's hard to believe that I am in Egypt with my husband, and it's been only one of many journeys in my life.

Maybe this new life you build for yourself and your child will be better than any you ever dreamed. Many of us have a plan about how our lives will go and it's good to have a plan, but life hands us lots of unexpected surprises along the way. When I look back on my life, I have been incredibly lucky. I've got beautiful successful children and grandchildren, have had a successful career, and have had many wonderful experiences and love in my life. Of course it didn't come without struggle and without hard work and help from people close to me.

I've done more than I thought I would in my life. I graduated from college. I've traveled to places I never thought I'd go like Europe, Egypt and Hawaii. I've met people I never would have met without having my child at such a young age. I might never have gone to college. I might never have become an author. For me, having another human being dependent on me, on what I did with my life, motivated me to accomplish things I never dreamed I'd accomplish. Challenge can bring motivation. No matter how tired you are, no matter how broke and broken-hearted you are, you can persist and move forward to a better place. You do need to know where you want to go in order to get there.

Where Do You Want To Be?

> *I am the master of my fate; I am the captain of my soul.*
> <u>Invictus</u> by William Ernest Henley

I have always been attracted to "rags to riches" stories. Novelist J.K. Rowling was a broke single mom on public assistance in England when she wrote the *Harry Potter* series. Who knows, maybe if she had a full-time job, she'd never have had the time or inspiration to invent Harry Potter while she was travelling on a train in England with her child.

I once worked with a guy in a wheelchair. He told me that in rehabilitation, counselors told him that there might be one hundred things he could no longer do, but a thousand things he still could. There are even a few things he can do now that he wouldn't have thought about doing before his accident. He was also the person who told me to only spend a limited amount of time on regret.

Having a child is a fortunate and happy event, but it might not seem like it when you're alone in the middle of the night changing diapers and feeding a crying baby. It helps to think about the bigger picture, that you're nurturing a human being, your own child, and someday your baby will be an adult. You baby is like a sponge right now, creating memories, listening to whatever you say, and learning by watching you.

There are times when you need to step back from your situation and assess it, decide where you are and where you need to be. For instance, you might want to move out of your parents' house, live in your own home, make your own money, and perhaps marry your boyfriend or meet the man of your dreams. When you look at how far you might be from that place, it can overwhelm you. Try instead to think of smaller goals and to appreciate the things you have right now, today.

The Big Picture

It helps to occasionally take a "birds-eye view" of your life: where you are and where you want to be. Take a few minutes each day to sit and meditate and let your mind zoom up to a bigger view of your life. When you see your life on a bigger scale, realize that this is a short time in your life. Your baby won't be a newborn forever and won't always be as demanding as he or she is right now. There are struggles ahead, but everyone has struggles. Your struggles are simply different from those of your friends. Your worries might be bigger, maybe more important now than what you'll wear to the dance, or who is dating whom, but this difficult time won't last forever. You'll find new joys and passions in your child and in your own life.

My husband is a fan of storyboarding. He's got a "vision board" on which he glues pictures of things and experiences he wants; a new house, a certain number of customers for his business, or success as an author. Most of the things on his board happen—because he makes them happen.

Act "As If."

> *"While trying to become an actor, I wrote myself a check for $10 million and wrote in the memo: 'For acting services rendered.'"*
> —*Jim Carrey*

Right now, society is "pro-mom" and we hear a lot about "stay-at-home moms" and about women who quit their high-paying jobs to be with the kids. But our society isn't perfect. It doesn't reward ALL moms. Just the moms that seem to be doing the right thing; being married, being a stay-at-home mom and having money. The irony is that it's easier to be a stay-at-home mom if you have money. I don't use the word "hate" often, but I hate the "mommy wars." I hate woman-against-woman and mother-against-mother game.

I believe it's best to "act as if" you're doing the right thing. Make the best decisions you can, then act on them, even if you're not confident in the beginning. Don't let too many opinions sway you from your goals and dreams.

Wayne Dyer came out with a book years ago; *You'll See It When You Believe It*. The concept is similar to lots of self-help books these days, including *The Secret*. Critics of this book said that the book proposes "wishing for something and it will appear." Wishing is good if it becomes a goal. You work toward goals; you don't work toward wishes.

The point of both these books, I think, is that you have to believe that something good will happen to you so that you will make it happen. If you don't believe it will happen, you'll never try. Graduating from high school and going to college is one example. You have to believe that you can do it first, and then you take steps to make it happen. You can believe that you can live on your own with your child and comfortably support the two of you, and you can take steps to make this happen. So, it isn't magic, it is your setting goals and seeing them through. It's one day at a time and the days are not easy. The trick is to push through it even when it gets hard.

Act stronger than you *feel*. You're going to need help, no doubt about it, but when you ask for help, do it with strength in your voice and posture, even if you don't feel it. It's easy to fall apart to show people that you need help, but believe me; it's easier for them to help you if you explain your situation to them. "Can you help in any way? I need help with babysitting so that I can finish my high school diploma. I don't want to put it off any longer." People don't respond to weakness and whining. It's just a fact of life. Their first instinct is, "well, she got herself into this situation, she can get herself out." If you approach asking for assistance with strength and reasoning, then people are more likely to help.

Personal Power

You can build your personal power and gain control of your life. Are you more powerful with a man or less powerful and capable if he leaves? Many young women want to "find a guy" who loves you and takes care of you and your child. I think it's built into our DNA to think this way. Most women want to feel taken care of even after we've built a career and are independent on our own. We want to feel that the man we're with is at least as competent and successful as we are. Since women mature emotionally and mentally ahead of men, chances are your teen baby's father won't be up to the task. Even if he's older than you, chances are he's not ready to support you and a child. That's why so many teen relationships break down. It's too much responsibility at too young an age. I see that now that I've been through it, but when you're there, all you can see is you and this guy making a family together. It works out sometimes, but the odds say no, it won't work out and you'll need your own personal power. This means earning power, emotional power, and personal power.

You can build personal power and future earning power with education and a clear plan for your future. I think hoping for a good strong relationship with a guy can be part of the plan, but it can't be the entire plan.

You can *feel* powerful by finding a powerful man or having powerful or popular friends. The best kind of power is personal power—power that you've created for yourself by building your self-esteem through accomplishment. This kind of power includes knowledge, proof of expertise (a degree or certification or experience), acknowledgment from other people of your accomplishment, etc. This is power that you have earned. This kind of power can't be taken from you. It becomes part of you, part of your past, and part of your future. Sometimes it takes years of trial and error and work to build personal power, but if you keep at it, personal power becomes part of you.

You may not have the life you thought you'd have, but it might be even better than you ever imagined.

Aim High

I knew I wanted to graduate from high school and college even though I was a mother very early. Many people told me that I couldn't do it. Now many women become doctors and lawyers and successful business women. And, they are mothers too. You have many opportunities available to you. You have many roads you can take.

If I could go back in time and talk to that younger me, I would tell her that she's going to make it. Not only that, her goals would exceed what she thought she could do. I would tell her not to allow anybody to stand in her way, to criticize her or her child, to harass her family, or to make or her baby feel inferior in any way. I would tell her that maybe she could have done more than she actually did, even though she did pretty well. I would tell her not to hesitate, not to doubt herself or her child.

How Will You Do This?

No excuses (I'm tired, I don't have babysitter, I'm poor, I don't have time, I'm a mother now, I'm too old). People have done harder things with fewer resources.

    A three column list works for goals: What, When, and How. If you do this on your computer, you can easily look at the goals every day. You can highlight the priorities. You can change them, but don't let them drop off unless you're sure it's no longer a goal.

Imagine a Bright Future

It's 1974 I go to a gymnasium at Colorado State University where I'm working and going to school part time. Gloria Steinem is speaking that day. None of the men seem to know who she is. Ms. Steinem was controversial then, having been quoted as saying "A woman needs a man like a fish needs a bicycle."

    In the seventies many women who went to college were there looking for educated and worthy husbands. Women were not usually allowed to buy houses on their own or have credit cards. Working women were expected to be teachers or nurses or airline "stewardesses" (a glamorous job back then). They were not expected to have lifetime careers or work outside the home if they didn't want or need to. The Viet Nam war was reaching its terrible end and the country was generally in upheaval. The "kids" of my generation were angry and rebellious. Streaking naked across campus and passing around marijuana at parties were popular activities. I was newly married—a marriage that was destined to fail but gifted me with a second beautiful daughter and much knowledge and understanding. I didn't know how much I would need the strength and reserve I soaked up from Gloria Steinem that day in the gym.

    *Gloria spoke to a half-full room that day; there were few men. She looked petite and glamorous in her Pucci psychedelic top, purple aviator glasses, and platform shoes worn with bell-bottom trousers. Her hair fell around her in a blond lion's mane, and she was beautiful. Her voice, unlike her message, was soft and monotone. I wanted to **be** her.*

    She spoke about her history: she graduated from Smith College with high honors; she won a grant to go to India where she witnessed terrible poverty and oppression against women; she had participated in protests; she had gone "undercover" as a Playboy Bunny and wrote an article about the bad treatment of the "bunnies"; and she'd become a household word with her association with the "Women's Liberation Movement." She was both beautiful and intelligent.

I was envious of her and at the same time intrigued and inspired. No, she wasn't a single mom, but she empowered women. Yes, she was considered controversial and was hated by many people. She and others were the beginning of more rights for women. They were more militant maybe because they needed to be to get attention.

Of course women need men. Of course marriage isn't bad. What Ms. Steinem and others offered were opportunities and alternatives. The women's movement would swing from one extreme to the other for two decades before coming to a semi-balanced position. The point wasn't to reject men in order to accept yourself, but to have the right to choose your own future, have the right to equal pay for equal work, to have control over your own body, and to decide if you wanted to marry or not.

The Vision

When I went to that speech by Gloria Steinem, I had taken a break from my on-campus job as a "data entry specialist." My then-husband was getting his Bachelor's Degree, a goal that I felt was out-of-reach for me. I lurked around in the libraries on my breaks, wishing I was one of the students.

After that day I imagined myself getting a Bachelor's degree and not just taking classes here and there. I imagined a career and I imagined myself being a published writer. I resolved my feelings of guilt and shame for having had a child without being married.

All of the things I imagined that day happened, not any because they came magically to me, but because I had a plan. It didn't go exactly as I planned. It took longer than I expected and was harder than I expected. I got more resistance from others than I expected. Not everyone was in my corner.

After I gave birth to my daughter I knew that I wanted to graduate from high school, and not just with a G.E.D. (not that a G.E.D. isn't a good option). When it came to going back to high school, and heaven forbid, to college; it's not that I couldn't do it; it's that *they* didn't want me to do it. *They*–teachers and school counselors, and parents of other students, and some of the students themselves. If I did it and was successful, it would violate their beliefs that I'd ruined my life, that I was destined to work at Dairy Queen (not that there is anything wrong with starting there). It violated their values, their world view, maybe even their moral compass. This doesn't make them bad people; there are many good people who still believe the same way. Mothers and fathers need role models for their daughters, and they don't want those role models to be teen moms.

The only way to get through this is to walk through the fire—straight through without looking at them. Walk through it and DO IT.

I think society today is a little more tolerant, maybe MUCH more tolerant. I got called out on the street, although I tried to ignore it. I'd brought a new innocent life into the world, someone who would one day grow up and finish college, have a stunning career, and a beautiful family. But the way people looked at us at that time, the way they stared, their eyes going first to my somewhat still-flabby stomach to my hand and then to the young daughter whose hand I held—the way they looked at us with disapproval, as if I'd killed someone or harmed them personally. I was afraid my daughter would see and internalize it as I sometimes did, but she did the opposite. Like a beautiful cat who persuades a person to love it, to pet it, she reached out to people. She was charming and witty and outgoing and still is. It is her gift and it would save her on many occasions.

One by one, I completed my college courses and got a Bachelor's Degree—free of charge by using free credits provided by my campus job. I later earned a Master's Degree—free of charge by using tuition aid provided by my job.

Wishes, Dreams, and Goals

"A journey of a thousand miles begins with a single step."
Confucius

Many of us wish that someone would give us a job, or a book deal, or a singing deal, or whatever it is that our hearts desire. But, don't discount your own talents and your own persistence. You have talent for something. Everyone does. Most of us won't have our dreams handed to us or a mentor come to us (as they do on some of the reality television shows), so we need to make it happen.

I spent some time thinking about the differences between having a wish, a dream, and a goal.

A wish is defined in the dictionary as "A desire, longing, or strong inclination for a specific thing."

The dictionary defines a dream as "a condition or achievement that is longed for; an aspiration." A different definition gives us "A wild fancy or hope." I choose the first definition because we hear enough of the second (as in, "You are wasting your time trying to be a singer.")

The conclusion I've come to is that a wish and a dream are similar; they both represent a desire for an achievement or outcome. We all have a need to feel important, to achieve and to be recognized for those achievements. We all want our parents to be proud.

If you've taken a psychology course, you learned about the halo effect and self-fulfilling prophesies. The halo effect means that because you've done something considered "good" by social standards, then you are "good" in all that you do. If you do something considered "bad," then other bad things are expected of you. So you can see that if your parents are disappointed in you for becoming pregnant, then they might expect bad things of you. They might not believe you'll finish school or become successful or be a good mother.

If you believe that you cannot finish school nor have a happy family or a good career, then it becomes a "self-fulfilling prophecy." Because you believe it, you don't even try. You make it true by not acting on your goals and dreams.

I also believe in *downward spirals*. A downward spiral is sometimes seen as a string of bad luck where continual "unlucky" or "unfortunate" things happen to a person. If you believe in *downward spirals* then you also need to believe in *upward spirals*. You can make good things happen to you, even if they are small. Sooner or later these good things will add up and increase your confidence, leading to an upward spiral. Certainly not all bad things happen all the time, nor do all good things happen all the time. Much of it is how you perceive things. Some people are sent "over the edge" by a flat tire on a car, while others handle serious illness with grace.

Action is what turns a wish or dream into reality. People who achieve their dreams set realistic goals and then act on those goals. Goals lead to action. Completion of a goal starts with a dream, but the dream is just the start. Most of us will have many jobs before we reach our full potential. If you have a job you hate and dread going to each day, think of it as a stepping stone, as experience. Most jobs give us something, whether it is learning a procedure or simply learning to show up each day. Nothing stops you from having a job to pay your bills and provide benefits for you and your child, and also fulfilling your dreams.

Here are a few guidelines for setting goals to lead to actions that will help you fulfill your dreams:

Set a Goal:

- Make it clear and well-defined.
- Make sure it is reasonable and do-able.
- A goal should be something you are passionate enough the create persistence.
- Be persistent about your goal.
- Set a deadline for your goal.

Achieve a Goal:

- Write down the goal and its due date, and read it every day.
- Do research on what you need to do.
- Be specific about how and when you will achieve the goal.
- Break the goal down into smaller goals.
- Read your goal list every day.
- Share your goals with trusted people.
- Work on your goal—don't just talk about it.
- Be persistent.

Rules for Wishes, Dreams, and Goals:

- Let yourself wish and dream. These thoughts and hopes help you define who you are and what you want out of life, as long as

these are positive thoughts and hopes. A positive dream might be to own your own restaurant, or to become a lawyer.
- Set your goals high, meet them. Then once you've met those goals, set new, higher goals.
- Don't let someone else talk you out of your dreams and goals as long as they are reasonable.
- Don't read too many celebrity news sites or watch too much "reality" television. This is a big "gotcha" for me. Comparing yourself to celebrities or other famous people makes me feel small and untalented in contrast. Look to yourself and how far you've come. This is called being "self-referential" instead of always comparing yourself to others and feeling inferior.
- Write your goals down and look at them every day. My husband keeps his goals in a place where he reads them each day and he also keeps a journal. I keep mine on my computer, but I've heard of people keeping them in their wallet.
- Give yourself small rewards when you achieve a goal. Or, better yet, announce your achievement so that others can help you celebrate.
- Talk to people about your goals, but only to those who are supportive. Don't talk about your goal too soon in case you change your mind or drop that goal off your list. Don't talk about it more than you work on the goal. As Yoda said, "Do, do not try." What he meant was, don't keep saying, "I'm going to *try* to go back to school." Just go back to school.
- Don't complain or whine to people. Sometimes it is human nature to be unsupportive and unsympathetic and you'll end up giving up on your goal. If you need to vent (and we all do), choose a trusted friend or another young mom, or a counselor to talk with. Instead of complaining, ask for help if you need it. If you don't get the help you need or want, think up alternatives.
- Get honest input from someone you trust with your dream. I'm a fan of the show Project Runway. On one show, one of the finalists made his garments partially from human hair. He was literally making "hair suits." When Tim Gunn got to him

to critique his work, he kept saying, "Oh my." By that time, the finalist was too far into his project to back down from his idea. The moral is to get honest input from someone you trust with your dream. This needs to be someone who is supportive, not envious, will not sabotage your efforts, but who will be completely honest with you. You may still create a few "hair suits" and some of them might fly, but getting input could save you some time.

How Can You Choose Success?

"Tomorrow is the most important thing in life. Comes into us at midnight very clean. It's perfect when it arrives and puts itself in our hands. It hopes we've learned something from yesterday."
John Wayne

I find that most teen mothers are an optimistic group. Teens in general are confident and optimistic about their futures (with exceptions of course—teen depression is also a problem). Sometimes that optimism enrages adults and others who feel we should be more humble, more sorry, more—something besides optimistic. People expect contriteness—being sorry. We can only say "sorry" so many times before it wears on us. But optimism will take you a long way to becoming successful, not only as a parent, but as a person. You're the same person you were before you had your baby; you've just got more responsibility now. That additional responsibility can translate to additional motivation. Sure, you'll be tired and get discouraged, but you're young. You can handle it.

Some of the qualities that will help you become successful are persistence, ethics, appreciation or gratitude, resilience, luck, and a strong self-esteem.

P.E.A.R.L.S.

Girls usually like pearls, so here are a few "pearls" to take with you on your journey to success. **Perseverance. Ethics. Appreciation. Resilience. Luck. Self-esteem.**

Perseverance

> *"What do you first do when you learn to swim? You make mistakes, do you not? And what happens? You make other mistakes, and when you have made all the mistakes you possibly can without drowning - and some of them many times over - what do you find? That you can swim? Well - life is just the same as learning to swim! Do not be afraid of making mistakes, for there is no other way of learning how to live!"*
> *Alfred Adler (Austrian Psychiatrist)*

It's no coincidence that persistence is the first on the list of helpful tools to help you succeed, because nothing can replace practicing, and not giving up, and trying and trying again until you succeed. Persistence just means not giving up on something you really want. You may need to tackle it in a different way than you did before, and maybe it will take longer—but maybe not.

Ethics

> *Watch your thoughts, for they become words.*
> *Watch your words, for they become actions.*
> *Watch your actions, for they become habits.*
> *Watch your habits, for they become character.*
> *Watch your character, for it becomes your destiny.*
> *Unknown*

Since I first heard the word "Karma," I liked both the word and its meaning, since it means that you get back what you put out into the world. If you're kind and generous, you are likely to attract kind and generous people to you. If you are bitter and angry, you're likely to draw things into your life to cause more bitterness and more anger. The golden rule is a good one: *Do unto others as you would have them do unto you.*

Appreciation (gratitude)

> *"Gratitude is like a muscle that needs to be used often. Even if a feeling of gratitude isn't there, practice helps. Practice brings about the sentiment. What we have to do is practice, and the feelings come afterward."*
> M.J. Ryan, author of <u>Attitudes of Gratitude: How to Give and Receive Joy every Day of your Life.</u>

I came to the idea of gratitude later in life. I'd always had a feeling of thankfulness for the smallest of things; a sunrise or rainbow, a person's kindness, a thoughtful gesture. But, sometimes I carried around a feeling of "quiet desperation." I stole this thought when I came across a poem by Henry David Thoreau: "Most men lead lives of quiet desperation and go to the grave with the song still in them."

I decided this thought described me. I felt always shadowed by a feeling that other people had more than I did, that they were better educated, that they had some secret key to life that I wasn't privy to. At times though, I felt that I settled for too little, that I needed another degree or I needed to work harder, or that I had made the wrong choices.

Now, I think *balance* is the key. Don't be so grateful that you become complacent and satisfied with not working or achieving or educating your children. But, don't fail to appreciate those small things and bigger things that truly bring happiness.

It helps to wake up every day and think about the things you have to be grateful for. Maybe it's your baby's health and your own health. Maybe it's the fact that your parents are helping you so you don't have to work quite as hard. Maybe you're grateful that your teachers seem to be on your side.

Oprah talks about keeping a gratitude journal, but if you're like me, journals don't work. If it works for you, keep a journal or keep a gratitude jar and get your child to keep one. Tell your child (even while a baby) how grateful you are that he/she has come into your life. You may not mean it every day, but some days you will mean it so much you'll want to cry. Tell your parents thank you for helping you. Tell everyone who helps you how much you appreciate it, no matter how small the help. They don't want flowers or things or money in payment—they want to be appreciated and thanked.

Resilience

> *"We can either watch life from the sidelines, or actively participate...Either we let self-doubt and feelings of inadequacy prevent us from realizing our potential, or embrace the fact that when we turn our attention away from ourselves, our potential is limitless."*
> Christopher Reeve

The Mayo Clinic defines resilience as the ability to adapt to life's misfortunes and setbacks. True resilience is more than that though. We've all heard about people that keep getting knocked down in one way or another and keep getting back up. There's an old saying, "it's not how many times you get knocked down, but how many times you get up."

I think true resilience means perhaps finding a different way so that we don't get knocked down so often. Maybe you keep getting fired from your jobs. Are you in the wrong job? A crisis or misfortune is sometimes life's invitation to examine *why* it happened and *how* it happened and correct the course your life is on.

Luck

> *"Luck is what happens when preparation meets opportunity"*
> Seneca, Roman philosopher, mid-1st century AD

I believe that you can put yourself in luck's way the same way some put themselves in harm's way. We all know people who seem to be unlucky. They lose job after job. They crash their cars or get lots of speeding tickets. Is this bad luck, or is it a person putting himself or herself in harm's way?

Many *lucky* people have worked hard to put themselves in fortune's way. Maybe they seem lucky to get a great-paying job, but most likely they went on numerous interviews and perhaps they have a college degree, or they know someone who knows someone (networking). Most people we consider lucky have had many setbacks and disappointments. They just never quit.

Self-Esteem

We hear a lot about low self-esteem, but it's more serious and complicated than it sounds. Low self-esteem leads to feeling of hopelessness, helplessness, ongoing depression, drug abuse, physical abuse, phobias—and the list goes on. Sometimes it starts when we are children and may or may not have anything to do with how our parents treated us. Usually it is a result of feeling devalued or not good enough for any reason. Maybe your parents treated you great, but you got negative feedback from other kids at school or other grownups. It might have been a single word or sentence about your appearance. Maybe your parents treated you differently than you brother or sister and that caused your self-esteem issues.

What builds self-esteem?—accomplishment on our own. This is where PEARL comes in. With persistence and resilience and a little luck and ethics sprinkled, you **CAN** achieve your goals and build self-esteem.

So, remember your **P.E.A.R.L.S.** No girl should leave home with them.

Act As If

Jim Carey, the actor, has often told the story about writing a check to himself for ten million dollars and keeping it in his pocket until he finally had enough money to cash it. This is one form of "acting as if." I first heard this technique while trying to overcome my phobia of speaking in front of groups. I was told to act as if I were not nervous. It didn't make me less nervous, but I believe it helped me to control my symptoms more effectively.

If there is one quick simple thing you can do every day to help boost your self-esteem and to push away feelings of helplessness and hopelessness, it is acting as if you're already successful, as if you're already the best mom ever, as if you will get through high school and college, as if you'll meet the right person…

There are many forms of "acting as if," but essentially, you are acting the part of something that you want. When you go on a job interview, act as if you're sure that you'll get the job. Dress as if you already have the job. If you want a college degree, act as if you know you'll get one. Take your entrance exams, sign up for classes; tell your friends and family you're going.

I believe the reason this works is because other people see you differently when you act with confidence and self-esteem. You're less likely to be told no. You're less likely to be on the receiving end of abuse if you act as if you will not tolerate it. People are more likely to look at you in a positive light. More importantly, YOU are more likely to stand up for yourself, to **Get On With It**

I've dabbled in writing all my life and have finished a few books. My writing career started out as a wish: I wish I could write a book. Sometimes I'd say, "I hope I write a book."

My husband, who is a productivity expert, is very good at just starting things. Just get on with it. He also uses what Anne Lamott, author of *Bird by Bird*, calls the "shitty first draft" approach (or SFD for short). This is where you just get something done on your goal each day. You have to know where you're going with it, of course.

The other technique he uses is BIC (butt in chair). Many of us, including myself, are somewhat or extremely distracted by social media, television, cell phones, etc. Some of us might need medication for this distraction, but most of us can control it ourselves.

Turn off the technology for a few hours each day. Give yourself quiet time (if it's possible with your baby). Make a list of what you need to do to meet your goal. If you need help knowing what to do, ask an expert or look online (okay, I guess you DO need your computer for that).

Hopes and wishes without action are just hopes and wishes. Goals + action = success.

What Falls Away

> *What falls away is always. And is near.*
> *I wake to sleep, and take my waking slow.*
> *I learn by going where I have to go.*
> *From <u>The Waking</u> by Theodore Roethke*

Roethke's poem is about loss and about finding a new way after a loss. He's saying that we all suffer loss, even as we gain new things and new people in our lives. When your life changes, as it does when you have a child at such a young age, you lose a few things or need to let go of a few things in order to change. You may experience loss of your relationship with the baby's father or other men in your life. You will experience loss of your "old life." You may experience loss of friends and even family members.

When you have a child you, it changes your life immensely and may change the entire course of your life. If you think of this as an opportunity, it can change your life in a very positive way. Think of it as a detour or a different fork in the road that leads to the same destination in the end. Having a child young is not a dead end. It doesn't mean throwing goals away, unless they become impossible to do with children. You wanted to join the Marines? Maybe that has to wait because you now have a baby to think of. The baby needs to be factored into each and every decision now. Or, maybe joining the Marines isn't out of the question because your parents are willing to watch your child while you are away.

Some goals are harder to achieve while raising a child. It's like trying to change a tire on a moving car. Maybe it means delaying the entire goal for a while, working on the goal more slowly, or changing the goal. For instance, if you've always wanted to be a rock and roll singer, have the talent for it, and now have a baby—it's going to be harder to achieve caring for a baby, and earning enough money for the baby. So, maybe that means having a "day job" and picking up singing gigs one or two nights a week as your baby's needs allow.

Ignore the Statistics

> *"There are three kinds of lies: lies, damned lies, and statistics."*
> Most recently attributed to Mark Twain

> *"Most people use statistics like a drunk uses a light post, for support, not illumination".—*
> Andrew Lang

Statistics frustrate me. It's true that a certain percentage of teen mothers do not graduate from high school, let alone make it to college. It's true that some teen moms have more than one child. Some teen moms turn to drugs and alcohol to dampen their pain and frustration. It's true that a certain percentage of teen mom's children become teen parents themselves, and that a certain percentage are poor and abused. Remember when you hear these statistics that it doesn't mean YOU. It didn't mean ME and it doesn't mean YOU unless you let it happen. You are in control of your own life. A statistic is not an excuse for not trying or for letting a perceived destiny lead you down a certain path.

So…

Don't feel obligated to keep yourself poor or to downplay success just because you are a young mom. Don't use your child as an excuse not to move forward. Get on with it. You are young and strong and you can do it!

Tools for Your Journey

- **Goals:** Write down your life goals and share them with your family. How do you want your life to go?
- **Dreams:** Don't give up on them, even if you have to change them a little. You want to be an artist? You can still work on your art while going to school and taking care of your baby. Carve out a few minutes each day to work on your dream.
- **Thank You:** Remember to thank those people who help you financially. Thank your parents for letting you live at home. Thank people who babysit for you or give you baby clothing.
- **Remember P.**E.A.R.L.S: Persistence; ethics; appreciation (gratitude); resilience; luck; and self-esteem.
- **Connection:** Find a group of people who build you up and who help each other. Remember your online community.
- **Ask for Help:** Ask your family for help and tell them exactly what you need to make your goals happen.
- **Take Responsibility:** Learn all you can and have a plan.

six

Boys to Men

My daughter is over a year old and I've graduated from high school. I'm attending college locally so that my mother can help with babysitting while I get my Associate's Degree. I feel successful because I graduated from high school, but when I compare myself to other girls my age, I feel like a failure. I didn't get a scholarship to go away to college, and even if I had, I wouldn't have been able to go. I wouldn't be able to join the Peace Corp—something I'd had in the back of my mind. I don't have a boyfriend and it doesn't seem like there is one in my future. Most girls I'm going to school with date and go to parties and college football games. I wonder if anyone will ever love me and my daughter enough to get involved with me. I worry about it, but I don't date because I don't have time and because I don't want to explain my situation to someone new. Still, it seems important that I find someone. I could end up alone for the rest of my life. Even though I have a beautiful baby girl whom I love with all my heart, a supportive family, and a few friends who stuck by me, I feel unlovable.

Your mom or grandmother or dad might call your baby's father a "boy" but at least physically he *is* a man. Man or boy, he deserves a chapter. Not for him necessarily, but for you. It helps if you understand the male mind and how it differs from ours. Men and women, just by virtue of their DNA, think and act and make decisions differently.

I saw a recent dog-training episode where the dog wouldn't do a thing without getting a chunk of cheese as a reward. The trainer had a saying, "the cheese is the reason." Sex is to men like cheese is to a dog. By that I mean that while women are driven more by our emotions and need for love, men are driven a little more by their need for sex and to "win." Using the "dog" metaphor, a dog may need you a little less once you give him his cheese. A man might need you a little less once you give him sex, while it seems you need him more, and in fact you can become obsessively needy and too attached to him.

Don't take me literally and think I'm calling him a "dog,", but young men are different both physically and emotionally. Women are driven by a need to belong and a need to be loved. Sure, we have a sex drive just as males do, but our reason for having sex is different than that of the male. Males are more governed by their hormones than we are. They are governed by an innate need to be independent and powerful and respected by their male friends. They are driven by a need for power and to conquer. Once they've conquered someone or something, the thrill is gone. Many women feel a strong emotional attachment to someone they have sex with. We have more attachment hormones than men do.

Boys usually get a different reaction from their friends when they're about to become a parent. They get a slap on the back (perhaps of congratulations) or a joking condolence. Many boys and men do step up when you announce you are pregnant and actually want to parent their child. Most of them don't know what that means on a day-to-day basis. Sometimes they'll say things like, "I'll bring over a box of diapers every now and then." Or, they might tell you that such a tiny baby couldn't cost that much or take that much time. After all, don't they sleep all the time? They may not have a good picture of the work, money, and time involved in raising a child.

Parenthood has joys, but it is also a long and relentless process. Parenthood brings rewards along the way when it is done right, but for a long while the work outweighs the reward. He needs to know and commit to what he's getting into if he is going to be an active father. I once worked with a guy who kept a child's picture on his desk. This guy was about thirty and the child looked to be about ten years old. I asked him who the child was and he said, "He's my son. He's ten." I then asked him about the boy; what he liked to do, what grade was he in, etc. He didn't know. He hadn't seen him since he was a year old. "You don't see him?" I asked. "No," he answered, "I plan to catch up with him when he's twenty or so."

I never saw the guy again; he moved to another company, but I suspect that when and if he caught up to the child there would be lots of resentment and anger and explaining to do. Still, many of you want the baby's father in your life. Some of you may have made the decision to keep and raise your child based on what you thought he wanted. Men are important to us. We need our father's love when we're children. We crave love and approval from men for most of our lives. We want to look pretty for them, to be sexy for them, to please them. We want them to love us. We want to draw power from them, and that's why women are attracted to powerful or seemingly powerful men. We want them to protect us and take care of us. Does that mean we don't want to be independent and take care of ourselves? No. Most of us want an education and we want to get recognition and power on our own, but we are still innately attracted to men who can give these things to us. Decades of gaining equality in the workplace and education and armed services haven't changed the nature of our relationships with men, except that it is easier to have our own careers and lives. But the desire to have a loving and stable relationship hasn't changed.

Many of the teen moms on the television show *16 and pregnant* and *Teen Mom* spend a lot of time talking about finding a man to take care of them and their child. *Where will I find someone to love me?* Many of them, even the ones surrounded by family and friends, still say they feel so *alone*. What they mean is that *he* isn't there. The one. Or, if he wasn't the one, there must be one. Mustn't there?

I saw a story on the news about a female astronaut who gave up everything to drive across the country stalking her astronaut boyfriend who had dumped her for another female astronaut. The urge to be with him, to win him back, to tear him away from this other woman, had caused her to throw away her reputation, her education, her career to chase him down. Of course, he didn't want to be chased. She probably knew it wouldn't end well, but her emotions took over and the rest was history.

What makes intelligent women do things like this? What makes us look on his phone for incriminating messages or go through his sock drawer for proof that he's cheating? What makes us give up our dreams and instead work full time on keeping him with us? What makes us stay with a cheating or abusive man? Many times we find the proof and ignore it anyway. Why? Why do women do this? I know that I've done it myself before I figured out what real and mature love looks like and feels like.

Even Oprah talks about stalking a boyfriend in her early years. I'm sure this guy has regrets now, but at the time, Oprah was a struggling and needy woman. Men become emotionally needy too, but usually it's the woman who gets so emotionally bonded to the guy that they think they cannot live without them. We look for reasons that he doesn't love us. Why do we do this? Do women have some sort of super instinct for cheating men? Or are we crazy stalking witches? We probably fall someplace in between.

Whether your baby's father is young like you or older than you, he may or may not be in this 100% with you. He may not be emotionally mature enough to stick around. He, like you, may not have known what he was getting himself into entirely and may start acting in ways that seem alien to you.

This may not be the best time to find a new boyfriend if your baby's dad isn't in the picture. This is the time to bond with a group of girlfriends—maybe not the same ones you had. This is the time to grow, to learn something new, and to work on your degree. This is your chance.

We are Loved If Our Children Love Us

I believe that while men might see children or babies as accomplishments (and sometimes they see the accomplishment as complete as soon as the child is born), women see children as extensions of themselves. We see the child as part of us, as integrated to us, and therefore all of us were abandoned.

It's important to understand this drive, this need to find another man to replace one that rejected us.

While I believe it's okay to date, I believe now that young women should put as much effort and time as they can into improving their own situation through education and improving mothering skills. It's important to build your own self-esteem and to realize that you can be successful on your own. It's easy for me to say looking back because I didn't always follow this advice. I spent more time away from my children than I needed to. I exposed them to more needless and empty relationships with men than I needed to. I probably put them in harm's way without meaning to or without thinking enough about it.

Some of us have trouble finding good female friends after we become mothers. Many young women don't really want to be around another who has a baby. It reminds them that they too could be in that situation. They might be afraid you'll ask them for a favor or that you are too needy. Evaporating friends might make you feel lonelier and more driven to find a new boyfriend.

Remember that as young as he or she is, your child loves you.

Things to Watch for in Baby Daddy

He didn't tell me how to live; he lived, and let me watch him do it.
~Clarence Budington Kelland about his father.

This sentiment says a lot. Children learn from what we and others tell them certainly, but they learn even more from watching the actions of their mom and dad, their grandparents, their siblings, and their friends. They watch from day one. Some young parents believe that young babies and toddlers don't know what's happening, but they do. If they hear daddy yell at mommy, they come to believe that it's normal. If they see mommy and daddy fighting, they learn to fight. Children do what you do, not what you say. This simple concept will take you a long way to being a good parent. If you don't want your child to fight, then you cannot fight with the baby's dad in his or her presence.

Does your baby's dad get agitated and upset when he's around the crying baby? Does he shake or begin to shake the baby? Does he storm out of the house (this is preferable to any kind of violence). Many, too many, children are killed or injured for life by shaking injuries. If he does this, make him leave or go to another room. Don't leave the baby alone with him because if you've seen him do it, then he'll do it when you're out of sight.

Does he act uninterested or disgusted by the baby? If so, he's probably not bonding. Some men bond with the child when he or she is older, but you must watch this closely. He may blame his lack of freedom and his lack of access on you or your child.

Does he neglect to help out financially and physically? This leaves the entire burden on you and your family (if they are helping you). You cannot do this alone. I didn't do it alone; I had my parents and brothers and sisters, and while it took me a little distance to realize just how much they'd done, they were there for me.

Passive-Aggressive Behavior

> *"Someone I loved once gave me a box full of darkness. It took me years to understand that this too, was a gift."*
> — Mary Oliver

One of the hardest things to do is break up with someone whom you deeply love. Maybe it's easier when they treat us very badly. It's more black and white than most relationships.

Maybe he isn't exactly abusive. Maybe he just seems distant at times or all the time. Does he run hot and cold with you and the baby? Maybe he picks a fight over the way you looked at him or the way you asked him to do something. Maybe he wanted to leave and be with his friends, so he argued with you to obtain an excuse. Some men get alternately mean and kind. He might get mean out of frustration, and then try to sooth his conscious by being kind. It's possible that part of him wants to stay with you and the baby, and part of him wants freedom and wants to stay young.

Some have a difficult time after a baby arrives. Most young men don't really know what they're getting into once the baby arrives. They might feel trapped and unable to cope but also unable to express how they feel.

They may feel jealous of your affection for the baby. They may look at you differently since your body has changed and it has changed to meet the needs of your baby, not him. Sometimes they don't know why they're acting the way they are. Some of them have affairs with other women, and strangely enough, some girls are attracted to men who have just had babies and are not quite committed to the relationship.

Passive aggressive behavior means that you can't quite say that he's abusing you. He hasn't hit you or shoved you or hurt the baby, yet. He might be acting like a jerk much of the time, and then when you've about had enough he will apologize. He might run hot and cold for you and the baby. This isn't all right. This behavior is still abuse whether he physically hurts you or not. If you're emotionally hurt or abandoned, it is abuse.

Does Pavlov Ring a Bell?

Back to the men-are-like-dogs metaphor. If you want the baby's father to step up to his responsibilities, *reward him every time he does something father-like*. The reward doesn't have to be anything big; it can just be a "thank you" or a hug. Blow him a kiss. Get him a cold drink. Little rewards lead to big changes in behavior, as long as you're consistent about giving them.

Stop yelling at him for *not* doing what he should; start rewarding him when he does anything right. Pretty soon, he'll start doing more things right to get a reward. If he does do something he shouldn't, just lean back, cross your arms and shake your head disapprovingly. He'll get the message.

Failure to Commit

Some girls try to hang onto their baby's daddy when she might be better off cutting him loose. It's common for young men to keep one foot in the door and one foot out. If you feel he's not committing to you and your child, you're probably right. There are young men (or older if your guy is older than you) who step up to the plate, but many do not. There are clues that he's not going to commit. He might come out and tell you that he's not ready or he's not sure. His actions show the truth. If he's not around much or you don't know where he is much of the time, he is non-committal. How long should you give him? Not more than a few months. If he doesn't commit right away, chances are he will never truly commit. Sometimes it's better to decide right away what his relationship will be to your child. If he really wants to be a dad, contribute financially, and contribute emotionally, but not to you, then you get to decide or let the courts decide how much visitation he gets. It's emotionally too much for most young women to see her baby's dad drive up with another woman to pick up her child.

It is usually a good idea to get a court order for child support and a good legal guideline of what visitation right he has now or will have. If he's not around at all, then it's probably not an issue, but if he is in and out of your life, then you need some kind of legal guidelines.

Of course, if he does have legal rights to visit your child, then you must abide by the law, but if he's left it wishy-washy, then you can govern your life and your child's.

Dr. Jekyll and Mr. Hyde

Does he act loving and happy sometimes, and then turn cruel and reckless? Does he act fine with your parents or his parents, but act badly around you and the baby?

He might think that he holds most of the cards now. You've had his baby and he hasn't had to make much of a commitment. Other girls might suddenly be interested in him. He might be confused or he might be trying to keep "one foot in the door" with you. Maybe he isn't sure this is a permanent relationship, but he doesn't want you to date anyone else either.

He might be physically abusive and then apologize or blame it on drinking or drugs. He might be okay for a while and then it happens again.

When this happens, point out his behavior and ask him what the two of you can do to get counseling or other help. Ask him if he knows why he behaves this way. If he storms out or blames you, then he might be wavering about the whole fatherhood thing.

Emotional Abuse

I've always been an easy-going person and sometimes too easy going. Because of this, people said things to me when I was a young single mom that hurt me, my kids, and my self-esteem. It wasn't until I was older and somewhat wiser that I realized that I didn't need to put up with the abuse. I learned that I didn't have to give personal details about my life just because people asked. I had to learn the difference between abusive comments and honest advice. No matter who the person is (friend, family member, teacher, doctor); you do not have to take abuse either physical or emotional.

You don't have to tolerate rude and crude comments. What is crude or rude? Suppose someone writes on a public chat site that you "put out" because you had a baby? What if your boyfriend calls you a bitch? Anything that hurts your feelings or your child's or makes you angry and feeling helpless, could be abusive.

Examples of emotional and physical abuse are when a person:

- Says anything to DEEPLY hurt your feelings or put you down: including your parents, your friends, you boyfriend. What might hurt your feelings? Being told over and over again that you've disappointed them, that they're ashamed of you, that you'll never get out of this mess (in short, anything that makes your self-esteem plummet).
- Hits you, pushes, shoves, or slaps you.
- Hits your child, pushes, shoves or slaps you child.
- Says mean things or demeaning things to your child or about your child.
- Tells you that you're nothing without them (this is usually a parent or a boyfriend). When you hear this, it is usually the person feeling more powerful than you because they know you are dependent. Situations like this usually escalate instead of getting better. There are exceptions if both of you get counseling to figure out why your relationship is deteriorating.
- Makes you feel inferior. Maybe your teacher puts you at back of classroom because you've had a baby. Maybe your boyfriend puts you down. Maybe your mother consistently rides you about being a bad mother.

What can you do when you're being abused or think you are? Often the people who emotionally abuse you are the people you're closest to or need the most. It might be a teacher or a friend. It might be your boyfriend or parent. Instead of fighting (which never works and always escalates abuse), calm down and cool off, then go back later and talk honestly with the person. Say, "Mom that hurts my feelings when you talk about me that way. It makes me cry and makes me think I'm a bad mother." Then walk away if the abuse continues. Repeat this as often as you need to. If you can put words around your feelings, it might help everybody deal with the situation better. If that doesn't work, try counseling. Counseling costs money, but there are organizations that will help. Maybe there is a guidance counselor at school (make sure he or she is good). I always tell people that just because someone has a degree or title doesn't mean he or she is good and has good motivations. If a counselor doesn't work for you, find another. Only you can decide who is good for you.

Malice in Wonderland

What if he really is abusive and you know it? If he hits you or emotionally leaves you feeling upset and crying frequently, if he shoves or threatens you, then he is abusive. Does he escalate discussions into arguments? Do you? Do you end of fighting most of the time? If so, this is an unhealthy environment for your baby. The baby will grow up thinking this is normal and will start fighting in school and grow up fighting with his or her partners.

Fighting and emotional abuse is never acceptable on any level. Ask someone for help. Ask him to leave if you are strong enough. If an argument or fight leaves you frightened, then you need to call the police. When you do this, you're setting up a record that he is violent. Be aware that if arguments and fights escalate to this level, then courts become involved. Usually someone is arrested or at least given a citation. It isn't always the male in the situation. Sometimes girls get caught up in violence and act on it against young men. This is just as much abuse as when committed against a girl.

Will he change? He might, but it may take years and he may not stay with you. Some men become different with some maturity and sometimes it takes a different woman for him to change. It's not that the woman changes him, but that he changes enough to have a different kind of relationship that's more mature and more equal. This hurts to hear, I know. Why can't he change for you? Some do, but it's rare. It takes a man maturing and going to counseling and understanding how to change a relationship. A relationship that starts when you're both young and evolves into an abusive one on either part (women can be abusive to men as well) is very hard to change. It's like adding a basement to a house that only has a slab foundation. It's much much harder than building the basement to begin with. Does that mean you shouldn't try? No. If he's willing to go to counseling and to work on the relationship, then it has a chance. But, can you make him change? No. It doesn't happen.

When to Let Go

Letting go is extremely hard, especially if you are in love with your baby's father. It probably seems impossible, or you try breaking up and keep going back to him again and again. Some young women become pregnant again between these breakups because they believe they are done with him (and other guys) and then he comes back again and you take a risk.

How do you know how many chances to give him? How do you know when and how to break up with him?

If he has persistently broken promises to you and your child regarding visitation, money, or other help, it might be time to let go. If you know he's dating someone else, it IS time to let go. If he's ever abused you or your child physically or emotionally, it IS time to let him go. If he is abusive to your family or friends, it is time to let him go. If he is abusing drugs or alcohol, it IS time to let go. If you are unhappy or crying much of the time over him, it IS time to let him go. If you are constantly checking up on him, suspicious of him, or worried about your relationship, it might be time to let him go. If your friends all tell you that he isn't good for you or that he's dating or doing other things behind your back, it might be time to let him go. If you cannot imagine the two of you together and working with each other for your child, then it might be time to let him go. If he tells you he doesn't love you, it IS time to let go.

How to Let Go and Handle the Emotion

Relationships don't always end quickly and cleanly. Sometimes couples do a "dance" of breaking apart and coming back together with each pass becoming more and more difficult. Some guys come back and act contrite for a while and then they get even worse than before. Maybe it's not just him or you but the two of you together. Sometimes it's so painful to break up that you end up making up and getting back together. For a while.

Don't let him drift in and out. It could last a very long time. Don't have sex with him (no booty calls). To women, sex = love. To men, most of the time, sex = sex. We get more bonded to a man we have sex with than they do. We take it to heart. Sex must mean he loves you, right? Not necessarily. Just save yourself the agony and don't have sex with him and certainly not unprotected sex.

What if he has visiting rights and no longer wants a relationship with you? If you can't handle him showing up to pick up your child, work something out with your parents or relatives so that he can visit your child at your house while you run errands or go to school. Ask him not to bring a girlfriend if that makes you depressed.

There are lots of ways to get over a guy, but the best way is not to think about him so much. Don't pour over pictures. Don't Tweet him or look him up on Facebook™ (or any other social networking site). Don't spend more than a few minutes a day thinking about him and what you could have done. Obsessing increases the desire to see him. Delete him from your email lists and phone lists.

Don't try to get revenge. Don't stalk him. Don't drive by his house or have your friends spy on him for you. Most women have done it. Even adult over-thirty women have done it. A rejection or breakup triggers some kind of obsession in us sometimes, but really, you can get over it. You need to get over it. In your heart, you know it won't work. It only drains energy that should be used for your child. This is hard for many girls who want "proof" that he's cheating or "proof" that he doesn't love you. *You already have proof if you doubt him. You already don't trust him.* The fact is, if you think he's cheating, he most likely is, or at the very least, you have a shaky relationship. Trust is one of the cornerstones of a good relationship. If you don't have that, then the relationship will not work anyway.

I watched Dr. Phil work with a young twenty-something woman, her husband *and* his girlfriend. The young man professed to love them both equally. They were both sleeping with him and evidently deadlocked about what to do. The married couple had a young son, which all three used as an excuse to bind the threesome together. In my mind, and evidently in Dr. Phil's mind, all the young wife needed to do was divorce, get primary custody, get child support, and go along her merry way. But, her emotions stopped her. She started bargaining.

Maybe I can live with this. Maybe we can be "sister wives." Maybe he'll get tired of her and come back to me.

Things don't usually magically turn around in a situation like this. It's the old "he's just not that into you" situation that spawned a book and movie years ago. It's sad sometimes but true. After the drama of a teen pregnancy, after all is said and done, he should love you more. Right? It seems that way, but in many cases he's just not ready. It's not that you're not good enough or pretty enough or smart enough. It's not that you're not enough. It's that HE isn't ready. He's immature. He's trying to get out of a difficult situation.

This is your chance to leave, take care of things legally, and use whatever support system you have to help yourself emotionally break away. Why? Because I'm telling you now that if you're experience this, you are being abused. It may or may not be physical abuse, but it is emotional abuse.

It hurts for anyone of any age to breakup with someone, but it's especially hard when you're young and maybe it's your first true relationship. It gets easier. The feelings will eventually change and morph into something else. You can thank him for giving you your child and let the rest go. Some day you may look back and realize that you made a better life for yourself and your child than would have been possible with him.

Dating Again

Don't rush into dating. You have a long life ahead and if you've got a chance to slow things down a bit, then take it slowly. Many young moms fear they'll never "meet someone." Sometimes this desire to have a boyfriend is because you're lonely or don't have a good friend system. Maybe you want to make your old boyfriend jealous or prove to your family that you can find someone who loves you.

I know it's easier said than done, but work on your school, your future, your baby, your family, your network of friends. If you rush into another relationship, it might not be much better than your previous one.

Here is a common scenario:

Julie was sixteen when she got pregnant with little C.J and seventeen when she gave birth to him. She struggled with the three options when she found out she was pregnant: abortion, adoption and raising her baby. Julie chose to keep her baby with her boyfriend Jasper's promise that he would stay with her always and they would raise the baby together.

Julie gave birth to C.J. and continued to live with her mother and sister. Julie loved her baby deeply, as did her mother and sister, but they all found caring for little C.J. harder than expected and the expense greater than they anticipated.

Jasper wasn't much help. He soon tired of hearing the crying baby and felt helpless to care for him at all. Julie and Julie's mother wanted him to get a job instead of going off to college as he originally planned. After all, Julie had to drop out of high school and put her diploma on hold, so why shouldn't he? Jasper's parents didn't want his future to suffer, so they urged Jasper to distance himself from Julie and C.J. He came around less and less and stopped offering money of any kind to help with C.J.

Broken-hearted, Julie began to yearn for Jasper to come back. After a year or so of fighting with Jasper and after he moved away, Julie began to date again. When C.J. was two years old, Julie met Connor, who was a couple of years older than she, had a good job, and seemed to love C.J.

Julie decided to move in with Connor with the blessing of her mother and sister, who were beginning to feel the strain of helping with C.J.

Connor seemed like a blessing at first. Julie began online study for her G.E.D., but Connor began to criticize her. What did she do all day besides watch a kid and do a couple of hours on her G.E.D. Connor began to feel more powerful than Julie and felt he should have more say in C.J.'s discipline and behavior issues. He felt C.J. had been spoiled and was too pampered. Connor became very strict with C.J. It began gradually: he had to finish his food before leaving the dinner table (even if it took hours); he cried too much and had to stifle it or be punished; and some things like sneaking into bed with mom or watching too much television became forbidden.

Julie felt guilty and trapped. C.J. wasn't happy. It seemed Connor didn't really like her any more. She couldn't afford to live on her own and her mother didn't want her to move back home.

Julie not only felt trapped—she was.

This happens more than we like to think. Men don't always bond the same way with our children as strongly or in the same way that we do. Men usually like to "fix" things they think are wrong or believe that things can be "forced" to make them the way they want. They want to fix our "spoiled" children or make sure they know who the boss is.

The best thing is to NOT move into a man's home with his promise that he'll take care of you. You need more than that. Marriage is good (if a little old-fashioned) because you are legally protected more than if you just move in with someone. A lengthy period of time before you make a commitment is good. It takes time to really know someone.

It's best to become as independent as you can for your own security. I always push education as a gateway to independence. Rely on your family if you can.

People, especially when we're young, tend to choose the same kind of person for a mate. It could be someone who subconsciously reminds us of our father or someone we admire. It might be the "bad boy" who attracts us. It might be a guy who seems to want someone to take care of him. Now's your chance to step back and compare the guys you've dated. Are they pretty much the same? Do they treat you the same way?

What About Sex?

Don't jump into another sexual relationship too soon. One study reported by the Center for Prevention & Early Intervention Policy indicated that one in four teenage mothers had a second child within two years of their first.

Teens usually don't want to plan sex because they may not intend to have sex. In most cases the couple gets "carried away" and either doesn't have birth control (condoms or other barrier method) available, the girl isn't on birth control, birth control fails, or the girl thinks she can "time ovulation." Timing ovulation and "pulling out" almost never work. Never have unprotected sex, not only because you can and will get pregnant if you haven't thought about it and planned for it, but also because the STD's out there today are life threatening.

The other reason not to hurry into another sexual relationship is that girls get emotionally hurt and involved much easier than the guy does. To you it might seem like the start of a relationship, but sex might just be a physical act to him. Women tend to bond more to a guy after sex because of estrogen and other hormones, but guys are "hard-wired" to have sex with many females. It's not fair, but it's fact.

Introducing Your New Guy to Your Child

Rule Number 1: make sure he knows about your child before you get serious. I found it hard to tell men that I had a child. Things might be different now and people are more open about having children outside of marriage and about single parenthood. I'm still surprised how many women hide the fact of their children until they feel the guy is appropriately "hooked."

This is wrong for you and for the guy and even more importantly, for your child. Maybe he'll "come around" or accept your children because he's gotten attached to you or you've already begun a sexual relationship. These relationships don't usually work because they've started out wrong. So, make sure he knows that you're a package deal right from the start! Just get it out of the way. The longer you wait to tell a secret, the more entrenched it becomes and the more damaging it is.

Rule number 2: Watch him carefully around your child. Is he good with him or her? Is he trying to take over discipline from you? Does he participate? How does he talk to you about your child? Does he admire you and your child?

Rule number 3: Run the other way if he's *too* interested in your child. If you ever get any nagging "red flag" feelings that he's way too interested in kids, he might be. Pedophiles are a reality, and it's becoming more evident that there are more out there than most women imagine. I heard one horror story about pedophiles hanging out in store baby isles waiting for needy-looking or single mothers. Pedophiles get good at meeting young children and will place themselves in situations to meet young children and spend time with them.

So…

There is the right guy out there for you and your child. You've got lots of time. Enjoy your status as a young person. Improve yourself and educate yourself so that you always have YOU.

Tools for Your Journey

Here are some things that might help besides just putting one foot in front of the other, doing what you need to do, and trying to stay positive.

- **Activities:** Make a list of activities you want to do with your baby or with friends...
- **Keep a Journal:** It helps to write down your feelings and reread to know your success or things you need to work on. If you are writing down more negatives than positives about the man in your life, re-evaluate it.
- **Get a Lawyer:** If you need child support or help with an abusive relationship, there are places that provide free or inexpensive help.
- **Thank You:** Continue to thank your "helpers." A simple "thank you" or "I appreciate what you're doing for me" goes a long way in soothing a difficult situation.
- **Ask for Help: Friends, parents, or counselors might be able to help if you've got concerns about your relationships.**
- **Connection:** Connect with other young moms. Every community has a young mom or teen mom program or high school. Even an online blog for young moms or a social media site can help.
- **Gratitude:** Minimize negative people and situations in your life. Have a gratitude list. Be thankful for those good things you have and the good things that will come into your life and your child's life.
- **Self-Talk: Keep your self-talk positive.** Don't say anything to yourself that you wouldn't say to your best friend.
- **Regression and Retreating**: If you think you're doing this, talk to someone about it.
- **Watch for Denial**: Do others tell you that you are in denial about your situation? Do you feel a sense of unreality or confusion? These are things to talk with a counselor or trusted adult about.

- **Snuff negative thoughts:** Try to recognize if you are spending too much time with negative emotions such as envy and jealousy, or anger. Measure your mood levels. Are you depressed?
- **Make new girlfriends.** Join or start a teen mom support group. Join an online support group.
- **Evaluate your relationships:** Look for signs of abuse or disinterest or signs that he's not going to work out. Use your support system to let

seven

Health Matters

Your most important job as a mother is to keep yourself and your baby safe and healthy. You will want to be physically healthy, drug- and alcohol-free and mentally healthy so that you can be there for your baby.

Your Physical Health

Pay attention to your own health after you have the baby. If you feel sick or have a fever, go to the doctor immediately. Sometimes infections or excessive bleeding require attention. If you don't have insurance for yourself or your baby, go to the emergency room.

If your baby has a fever, is overly fussy, won't eat, or has trouble with bowel movements or urinating, get him or her to the doctor immediately.

Don't worry for the first six weeks about your pregnancy weight gain. Some of it will fall of naturally, especially if you breast feed. After six weeks or whenever your doctor gives permission, you can start exercising. You can walk with your baby if you cannot steal an hour to go alone. Exercise videos are good. Weight lifting or treadmills or other exercise equipment is good, but many trainers user good old fashioned exercise using your own body weight, such as lunges, sit-ups, planks, etc. Exercise can help your mental attitude as well as help you to get you body back.

It's important to make sure your body responds normally after you have your baby. There are lots of books and information online to help you (just don't get too caught up in self-diagnosing). Some young mothers quit going to their doctor appointments because of money or health insurance concerns, or because of fears they have about doctors or being judged.

It's easier to keep scheduled appointments than to quit going, skip appointments and then have to start over with a new clinic or doctor. If you have insurance or money concerns, try a free clinic or even an emergency room if you've got a concern such as bleeding, infection, breast issues or anything that doesn't seem right to you.

Make sure to eat properly and drink enough water, especially if you are breastfeeding. Fresh foods are best. Fast foods have lots of salt and fat in them, so even though they might be quick and easy, they aren't the best for you and the baby. Try to get fresh fruits and vegetables and simple proteins (eggs, beef, chicken, and tofu).

Don't try to get your "real body" back too soon after you have the baby. Plan on six weeks to let your body repair itself and to let your uterus shrink back to its pre-pregnancy size.

Birth Control

You became pregnant once and it can happen again. Maybe you're not with your baby's daddy anymore or only see him occasionally. Maybe you don't date currently, but sometimes people get caught up in the moment and have sex when they hadn't planned to. Don't get caught unprotected! If there is any chance that you might have sex, it's better to be on a barrier or hormonal method if your body tolerates it, and always carry condoms with you.

Many women think that if they are breast-feeding, they are protected against pregnancy, but it isn't true. While it is true that ovulation might be delayed while breast feeding, there is no guarantee that you won't ovulate.

I know that birth control isn't free and it can be expensive. It is much less expensive than a child. Look at it that way. Raising a child to adulthood can cost $250,000; so condoms or birth control pills are an affordable alternative. Go to a local Planned Parenthood or free clinic if you cannot afford birth control or if you think your insurance won't cover it. Some teens say they use birth control *sometimes. Sometimes* we ran out of condoms. *Sometimes* she forgot to take her pill. *Sometimes* she wouldn't go to the clinic to see the doctor. Pregnancy is possible each and every time you have sex.

Another factor for some young women is that they still live with their parents or grandparents or other relative. Maybe your mother has become hyper-vigilant about knowing your business and who you're with and whether you might have sex again. Most parents say they want you to stop having sex and they might even ask if you've learned your lesson. This might prevent you from getting birth control so that a parent doesn't find out. My first line of advice is that if you feel safe confiding to your mother (or sister or grandmother), then tell them you'd like to be responsible and protected "just in case." If you know this won't go over or fear outbursts, then try for a "barrier" method such as an inter-uterine device or a shot that can be administered every few months. More important than confiding is being protected, even if you do so privately.

What about abstinence? While most people believe that NOT having sex is the best for your physical health and to prevent pregnancy, but unless you're absolutely sure and unless you never drink or do drugs and other risky behavior, it could work.

I personally don't think we should put sex in the same category as, for instance, drugs and alcohol. Almost every adult human has sexual urges. We have more of a choice about whether to use drugs and alcohol. We also choose when and where to be sexually active, but chances are if you've been having sex, you're unlikely to stop. If you chose abstinence, that is the very safest choice in terms of repeat pregnancy or STDs. But, be sure before you go without birth control.

If you've got a new boyfriend or are with the baby's father, there is a risk you could fall back into sexual behavior. It is, after all, part of what makes us human. Sex isn't just a moral decision; it is part of who you are as a sexual and emotional being. Like eating, which is a physical need, so is sex. Like friendship, the need for the comfort of a loving partner is a desire and a drive. Like eating, appetites can rule our behavior, and sometimes all the will-power in the world doesn't prevent us from eating—or from having sex. Be prepared. Don't leave it up to the guy because they don't always think ahead and they may be embarrassed or too cheap to buy condoms. I believe girls usually have more courage when it comes to asking for embarrassing things (could it be from buying tampons?), and so it might fall on you to protect yourself. Sure, you're protecting him too, but if a relationship develops, or AS it develops, you can become more open and communicate your concerns with your partner.

Many unintended pregnancies happen in between relationships or after a relationship ends. Maybe you decide to throw away your birth control or go off it and then in a moment of passion, you have unprotected sex. Some girls feel that they might be "slutty" by staying on birth control. You're just being smart and protecting yourself and your child.

Drinking and Drugs While Parenting

Of course you realize that drinking and drugs are a bad idea when you have a baby, but many young people get into a cycle of "self-medicating" with alcohol and drugs. Some young women never stop using drugs such a marijuana, cocaine or pills during pregnancy. You shouldn't breast feed if you do drink or use drugs, even occasionally. The baby is also using when you breastfeed.

If you're addicted, then you know that if you don't use you'll feel physically bad and mentally bad. This makes quitting even harder. You can't quit by yourself, so get help at an addiction center or simply tell a teacher or a parent that you need help. If your family and/or friends continually tell you that you need help, please listen. If you're addicted to drugs or alcohol, the chances increase that you may lose your child, get into legal problems, hurt someone else or hurt your child. Not to mention that any problems you add onto being a single mom will decrease the possibility that you'll be able to continue school, get an education and truly become independent.

If you've watched MTV's Teen Mom series, you've seen Jenelle and her struggle to overcome marijuana addiction. It seems that whenever Jenelle is deprived the opportunity to smoke pot, she gets belligerent, neglectful, and cannot concentrate on school.

So, be aware that every drug has side-effects, sometimes serious and sometimes minor that affect you and your baby.

Many teens today are given medications to help with anxiety and depression. My advice on using these is to "be slow to start taking prescription drugs, but be cautious trying to stop them." For instance, "benzos" that are commonly used to treat anxiety, are quickly addictive and can be hard to quit. They should never be stopped suddenly, as illness and even seizures and death have occurred.

Emotional Health

> *"At first I thought what I was feeling was just exhaustion, but with it came an overriding sense of panic that I had never felt before." Brooke Shields from her book,* Down Came the Rain

Many new mothers have "baby blues" and have occasional crying jags or feelings of depression. Be alert though for signs of Postpartum Depression, which is "baby blues" on steroids. It's dangerous for you and your baby. If your depression morphs into something worse or others are commenting on it, ask for help from a trusted adult or your doctor or counselor. Signs that your baby blues are more serious are things like inability to sleep or sleeping all the time, extreme sadness that goes on for longer than a few weeks, having fantasies about harming yourself or your baby, hallucinations, bizarre thinking, paranoia, mania, or suicidal impulses.

Don't get overwhelmed by the number of things you need to do. You can do them all, trust me. If you can't get them all done, do the most important things first. Whatever falls away may not be that important. Sometimes it's hard to recognize when we've gone "off the rails," so rely on friends or parents or teachers to help you. If they continually say they are worried about you, for instance, or if you're sending strange Tweets or E-mails to them, listen! Leave your child with someone where he's safe and get help from a doctor or clinic.

Anti-depressants are sometimes prescribed for "baby blues" or postpartum depression. They take time to work and they cannot be stopped suddenly. Many women pull out of "baby blues" on their own or over time once they recognize the symptoms; crying spells, feeling "out-of-body," feeling despair, feeling helpless and hopeless, and sometimes physical pain. There is a difference between "baby blues" and postpartum depression.

Some teen moms even suffer from Post Traumatic Stress Syndrome (PTSD). So, if you've got other problems that might be made worse by your experience, discuss these with your doctor. If he or she brushes you off or ignores your concerns, keep searching for help from other sources: books, online, other doctors, or alternative treatments.

It's sometimes hard to diagnose yourself, but certainly if you've had thoughts of suicide or thoughts of hurting your baby in any way, then you need help.

Confide, Don't Hide

I like to think that every person has someone with whom they can confide their most terrifying thoughts, but sometimes our instinct is to hide, not confide.

For instance, maybe you're afraid you are pregnant again. Or, maybe you *know* you're pregnant again. Or maybe you have a problem with drugs that you're afraid will be found out. Secrets are usually toxic. People keep all kinds of secrets, whether it is about sexual orientation or pregnancy, or drug use, or a traffic ticket, or a big money secret.

The less stress you have right now the better. Talk to someone. Confide in someone. Sometimes those closest to us are the hardest to confide in. We don't want to disappoint our partner or our parent. Maybe you feel you've caused enough "trouble" and don't want to hurt anyone again. Maybe you fear a lashing if you confide.

There is a well-known author who confided in a weekly column that she sometimes loved one of her children more than the other. She really caught criticism for saying it. Parenthood isn't all giggles and fun. Sometimes every parent thinks of running from responsibility, if even for a day or an hour.

Things serious enough to confide:

- Abuse of any kind to you or your child.
- Pregnancy.
- Drug or alcohol problem.
- Feelings that you might hurt yourself or your baby.
- Money problems.
- A secret relationship.
- Feelings that you are out of control.
- Grief or ongoing intense sadness over a breakup.

There are others, but remember you're not alone. If the first person you confide in cannot help you, then try someone else.

Never Leave Your Baby Alone

Years ago I read a story in the newspaper where a young mother needed to run to the store to buy milk for the baby. She didn't have anyone to watch the baby and so left her with her trusted German Shepherd dog. Unfortunately, the dog killed the baby. Never leave the baby alone (with or without pets). There could be a fire. The baby could fall or smother.

Never Shake a Baby

And, never shake your baby. Most of us know that babies are fragile and that shaking them causes brain damage. You wouldn't have to shake a baby very hard to cause injury. If your boyfriend, brother, mother, or anyone has a short fuse around children, don't leave your child with him or her. If you feel frustrated sometimes, leave the baby in his or her crib or with a safe person. Walk away and calm down. Many times we see in the news that a "shaken baby" was injured by a babysitter, boyfriend, or someone whom the mother left baby with.

Never Leave the Baby in a Car Alone

Most of us have heard stories about babies dying after being left in a hot car. The one that sticks most in my mind was the case of a well-respected teacher (not a teen at all, but in her thirties), who left for work, stopped at a bakery to buy donuts for the other teachers, went to work and forgot to drop her daughter off at daycare. The baby, left in the hot car all day, perished.

How does a mother forget her child is in the car? The entire country argued about whether she was a "monster" for forgetting her child in the car. How could donuts be more important than her baby? Honestly, I can imagine how it happens.

Mothers work these days. Sometimes both parents need or want to work. Combine frantic schedules with trading days dropping off and picking up the children, keeping sleepy babies in the back seat (out of sight for the most part) and I can see how it happens.

How to prevent these kinds of tragedies? Double check if you're trading off daycare duties. Call to make sure the baby made it to daycare if you didn't drop the baby off. Make it a habit to always look in your backseat as you lock your car. Leave yourself a note when you have the baby in the car. I know it sounds crazy that you'd have to remind yourself that you've got the baby in the car, but it isn't. And, never leave your baby in the car alone. We've all heard of car-jackings. Some of us have cars that lock themselves if the engine is running and the doors are closed. Don't leave your baby just to run into the convenience store. Not even for a minute.

Never Leave Your Baby with Someone You Don't Know Well

Use your instincts. I don't know if it's Urban Legend, but I've heard of pedophiles (guys who like children sexually) hanging out in stores looking for single mothers with babies. My rule is that if a guy loves babies too much, something might be amiss. I know it sound cynical, but better safe than sorry. Most young men and even older men care much more about YOU and about what you can do for them than your child. If he shows way too much interest in your child (above making you happy), then you might be suspicious. You can look him up online on a sexual predator website. Never leave you child alone with someone you don't know well.

Clothing and Other Things

Babies don't need the latest fashion, but they need to be comfortable. They need clothing that isn't too tight or binding and clothing that is appropriate for the climate you live in. Babies outgrow things very quickly, so try to buy a little bigger than your baby's current size. There are lots of places to get nice almost-new or new clothing without paying a fortune; garage sales, department store sales, clothing exchanges online, etc.

Medical Care

How do you know if your baby is ill? Be vigilant. Most women are, but sometimes we miss the signs of serious illness. Have a few basics: a baby thermometer, a baby scale to weigh your baby, a baby care book or a good website, perhaps some baby Tylenol™ for fever.

Use your intuition. Trust your feelings and your relationship with your baby. My young daughter contracted meningitis at the age of 1 ½ years. I took her to the doctor twice, and was told she had the flu (a flu epidemic was going on at the time). My gut told me that something wasn't right, that it was more than the flu, but I wanted to trust the doctor. Thankfully it was caught in time and she survived, but her hearing was damaged.

Doctors aren't perfect. So, even if you have to find another doctor (second opinions are good) or go to another clinic, follow your instincts if you don't agree with the doctor.

Get your child immunized on schedule. There is some buzz about immunizations causing Autism. Maybe it's true and maybe it isn't, but the statistics tell us that kids are in more danger to themselves and other children by NOT being immunized. If you're scared, ask the doctor for an individual dose (instead of "cocktails" that combine several immunizations into one). That means they can separate the different vaccines and give it in maybe three different doses instead of one big one. Ask the doctor if you can safely spread the immunizations farther apart. If the doctor acts like you're crazy or stupid, find another doctor.

Baby Furniture and Car Seats

Babies and youngsters under the age of five don't need that much. They need a safe and legal car seat. If you don't have one, check with local hospitals, thrift stores or look online for a good used one. They need a safe crib to sleep in. Don't put a lot of stuffed animals and blankets in your baby's crib. The less, the better. Experts now say not to take a baby to bed with you (you might accidentally suffocate him or her). However, we've all done it; fallen asleep with the baby in bed with us. Use your good judgment. If you don't feel your baby is safe in bed with you, always use a chair or rocker when you get up to feed the baby.

Other Considerations:

Get to know the "benchmarks" and make sure your child is making them. You can ask your doctor or lookup online what your child should be doing and when. If you feel something is "off," ask your doctor.

Take your child to all recommended physician's appointments.

Never water down formula or try to save money on baby food. If you don't have money for formula or baby food, contact your local food bank for help.

Go easy on the candy and sweets. You'll save yourself money in dentist's bills (not to mention saving them from the pain of cavities).

Go easy on juice drinks and sodas. They are full of sugar—ten teaspoons in a single can

Keep your environment as neat and clean as you can for you and your baby. This helps not only your health, but your emotional health.

Keep food simple and nutritious. Make sure you and your baby get an appropriate amount of protein, vegetables, fruit, and dairy. Try to make your calories count. If you keep your food as fresh as you can, you'll be doing great. Use fresh fruits and veges when possible. Watch for food allergies. Fast food is okay sometimes, but not appropriate for each day. Use fast food as a special treat.

So…

I believe that being a mother is the hardest job on earth. At a very young age, you are suddenly responsible for another human being, for what kind of person he turns out to be, for how healthy she is and for what memories he has. I don't want you to be afraid, but aware. Health and life are sometimes fragile. You need to weigh each decision you make from now on against the risks you take. It's a hard and enormous job, but you can do it.

Tools for Your Journey

- **Health:** Start a simple notebook with details of your baby's health and eating habits. Look at it at least once a week to see if you baby is progressing and growing.
- **Keep Your Baby Safe:** Never leave your baby alone. Never leave your baby in the car while you run into the store. Never shake your baby. If you are angry or frustrated, ask someone to take over or put the baby in his bed and give yourself a time-out. Never trust someone you don't know with your baby.
- **Keep a Journal:** Write down your emotional and medical concerns in your journal.
- **Thank You:** Continue to thank your "helpers." A simple "thank you" or "I appreciate what you're doing for me" goes a long way in soothing a difficult situation.
- **Ask for Help:** Don't hide. Confide. Ask for help going to or paying for a doctor.
- **Connection:** Connect with other young moms. Share you
- **Gratitude:** Be grateful for your good health and your child's good health.
- **Self-Talk: Keep your self-talk positive.** Don't say anything to yourself that you wouldn't say to your best friend.
- **Regression and Retreating**: If you have a drug or alcohol problem or if someone tells you that you have a problem, get help.
- **Watch for Denial**: Do others tell you that you are in denial about your situation? Do you feel a sense of unreality or confusion? These are things to talk with a counselor or trusted adult about.
- **Snuff negative thoughts:** try to recognize if you are spending too much time with negative emotions such as envy and jealousy, or anger. Measure your mood levels. Are you depressed?
- **Connections:** Talk with your friends about your child's development and health. Sometimes it helps to compare. If something is way off, ask your doctor.
- **Evaluate your relationships:** If you don't like your doctor or medical center or if they don't listen to you, find another doctor.

eight

Money Matters

Money makes the world go around—from the musical Cabaret

Money Basics

I'm sitting in my kitchen opening my mail. My oldest daughter is eleven and the youngest is two. I've been recently divorced, having been married since my oldest daughter was four. I'm crying as I open each envelope, each one containing a bill that I know I will need to stretch to pay. One is a surprise; a medical bill that is larger than expected. I begin to cry. My oldest daughter, the one I have trained to be stoic and strong, says, "Don't cry Mom."

I'm not crying about the one particular bill, of course, but all of it piling up around me. I have to remind myself that I've got a good job and good medical coverage. I have recently graduated from a four-year university. I get child support. I have no debt except for my home. Still, I'm overwhelmed.

I didn't know how lucky I was.

I lived with my parents until my daughter was four years old, and they never asked me for rent or money for food or any other expenses. They were not wealthy and had seven children, mostly younger. I worked while finishing high school and getting my first degree (a two-year Associates), but the money I made I spent on clothing and other things for myself and my daughter.

I never fully appreciated my parents' generosity until I was older and struggling a little with finances. I don't think I ever thanked my dad, and I know I would not have made it without him and my mother.

My children worked hard. They both worked through school, especially my oldest, who worked half-time during school and full-time during the summers. They both worked through college. I don't think it hurt them, but given a choice, I would have made their childhoods easier. If you ask a pregnant teenager what her biggest problem is, she might say her relationship with her boyfriend or with her family. She might say that her biggest problem is losing her friends or her former lifestyle.

What most teen mothers don't realize (as I didn't) is the monumental expense of having a baby and raising a child. For most teen mothers other people shoulder the burden; their parents, their grandparents, a little help from the baby's father or family, or help from non-profit or governmental agencies. Most teen mothers don't realize that one of the biggest problems they will face is MONEY.

What Does a Baby Cost?

If you search "how much does it cost to raise a child" on the internet, you'll get a number of calculators to tell you. It depends on many factors; where you live, how many luxuries you give your child, your own income, other children in the family, and many others. The number you come up with will be between $200,000 and $400,000 to age 18. That doesn't include college. The amount is staggering.

I can tell you though that I didn't spend what I was told it would cost to raise my baby because my parents shouldered the cost until my daughter was almost four years old. That isn't unusual (thank you all the accidental grandparents out there).

My children didn't have luxuries like the latest clothing and all the lessons I thought they should have. They didn't have private schooling and they both worked through college.

If you're living at home and considering getting your own apartment or making it alone, consider all costs. There are daycare and medical expenses, medical insurance, food, utility bills, rent. That doesn't include clothing and toys and a ton of other things you need or want for yourself and your child. There are always those unexpected expenses that can knock your budget right off its rails.

Pull a calculator off the internet to help you write a budget so you know what it will really cost to move out or to be on your own with your child. You need to add 10% for the unexpected. If your baby's daddy is helping, then you can do this together. Many teens are afraid to know how much it will cost. Do it once and then put it aside to let it sink in. Knowing is power.

This isn't to scare you, but to make you realize that you'll need to make your income as high as you can to give your child a better life.

More Money

I like to listen to money expert Susie Orman. She's got a lot of good tips about money and about getting out of debt and staying out of debt. Look her up online or in the library. She has a lot of good tips about money for women. One thing that always bothered me about her advice and books though is that little is said about *making more money*. Most money advice revolves around ways to eliminate and minimize spending. *Don't buy that cup of coffee don't get your nails done too often.* These are good tips, but what people really need to know is how to make MORE money. Women (and men) need to know how to increase their earning power, how to leave a low-paying job for a better one, how to get free education benefits, how to start their own business, and many more things that will put them in a better situation.

When I first met my husband, he had a mantra, "more money." He'd say it almost every day. It led him to make *more money* while working for a corporation and then later to starting his own business. I haven't heard him say it for years, maybe because he hasn't needed to. He has more money than he ever thought he would. It's good to have a mantra that you say to yourself every day to inspire yourself.

Should You Sacrifice Your Dreams?

Teenagers now, more than any time in the past, realize opportunities that match their dreams. They see reality shows where "ordinary" people become rich and famous overnight just by "being themselves."

They see people win the lottery or win a talent show or make a video and suddenly become rich and famous.

These things do happen, of course, but will it happen to you? There is a difference between having a dream and wishful thinking. The difference in how it turns out is action. Do lucky things happen to people? Do people win the lottery or get their own television shows? Maybe, but maybe not.

I remember watching an Oprah show and her guest was a weight expert. Oprah, who has always struggled with her weight, was at a heavy time in her life. Oprah told the man that she wanted to be one of those "skinny girls who never has to worry about her weight and flips her long pony-tail around her slender frame." The expert said back to her, "Yes, but you're not one of those girls. It's wishful thinking to believe you are."

I think about that every once-in-awhile. I want to be one of those people who write a novel and it becomes an instant best-seller, leading to more and more bestsellers. Is it okay to have this dream? Of course, and I will continue to write and work on my dream, but it isn't my "day job."

Most of us can have a dream and a profession. We can be a dental hygienist and create music videos on the side. Some of us will hit it big and others won't.

Be realistic. But, don't let someone tell you to let go of your dreams. It's okay to dream and to work on your dream. Don't give up the things you love. Fit your guitar playing and dancing into the time you have left after baby care and after school work.

I like to think of this as having parallel goals. A profession and a dream. Einstein was a postal clerk while he worked on his theories of relativity. Harrison Ford was a carpenter while he pursued acting in Hollywood.

Maybe you want to be a world-renowned chef or a television chef. Start with culinary school. Then, find out what it takes to work your way up in the chef profession. Find out what it takes to be a television personality. You may need acting classes. You may need to read all you can about how to become a famous chef. Before you become rich and famous (and in America, it can happen, right?), you'll be able to support yourself and your child.

I find it helpful to write down my goals and look at them every day. It's also helpful to get advice from supportive people. You need someone you can trust to give you honest advice and advice without judgment. For instance, your parents may tell you that since you've gotten yourself "into a situation" you can forget about that singing goal or the goal of going to college. A better approach is to find out *how* you're going to achieve your goal, then start doing it. Join a support group (of people who want to be chefs, for instance). Read helpful online blogs and talk to people who have done it. Your family and friends and even sometimes your school counselors may be less-than-positive about lofty goals. Say it to your baby. "I'm going to be a famous chef one day and have a published cookbook." Or, "I'm going to be a singer and sell a record."

My husband once told me not to tell everyone that I was working on a novel. Otherwise, people will continually ask you, "Haven't you finished that novel yet?" It slows down your progress because you just know those people don't think you'll ever finish it.

So, you don't need to sacrifice your dreams. You've just taken a little side-street on the way to the city of your dreams. Don't give up on yourself or your dreams.

Getting Help

Neither a borrower nor a lender be,
For loan oft loses both itself and friend,
And borrowing dulls the edge of husbandry.
Hamlet Act 1, scene 3, 75–77

Your parents and his parents and your immediate family might be your first line of help. Having a place to live with free rent and utilities and food is a big deal. Don't underestimate the cost of these things. It might be a pain to live with your parents or other family, but if they're letting you and your child live with them, it's a sacrifice for them too. In fact, you probably don't realize how much these things add up: groceries, baby supplies, heat and lighting costs, insurance, clothing, entertainment, and more. Your parents might be paying for more than you realize. Accept their help, but do it with grace and gratitude. Did I always accept my family's help with grace? No. I regret not thanking them and arguing with them over responsibilities and babysitting.

Child support

Don't be afraid to file for child support. It's not for you; it's for your child and it's for 18 or more years. If you don't get child support established right away, it will be harder if you decide to do it in the future. If your child's father is young himself, he might not make that much money. That's okay. The court takes that into consideration. It might not be much, but it will be established and once the father is making more money, your payments could increase.

Some girls are afraid of driving him away by threatening him with child support. The truth is that if he intends to stay and help you, he will. Child support won't drive him away. If he leaves, it will be for other reasons.

Public support

There is a common belief that most teen mothers end up on welfare. In fact, there are statistics that anywhere from 50% to 80% of women who became pregnant as teenagers end up on welfare. I believe that it's harder for single women in their twenties to support their children because they're on their own. They may not have the support of family or the baby's father. I never went on public assistance because I never needed to. My family supported me and then I was able to get employment with education benefits and medical benefits.

Teen mothers who live with their parents probably don't qualify for welfare in many cases, if the parents have a home and they have jobs. That's where education comes in because if you use these teen years to get your education, then you're less likely to need public assistance. It seems hard to go to school when you have a baby at home, but the best time to get your education will be when you've got an inexpensive place to live and people to help you with babysitting.

There's nothing wrong with public assistance or welfare to get you through a crisis or for a short-term when you need the help. The problem is getting off public assistance. Some women end up in a double-bind. If they get a job, then they don't qualify for the money they need to feed their family. If they make too much or own a house or anything valuable, then they may lose their public assistance. The problem with this is it can make you stuck. Whatever dreams you're trying to pursue can become sidelined by trying to stay on public assistance.

I like assisted education projects, so if you can get funded to attend school, take full advantage of those benefits. If you can get health care through public assistance, then take advantage.

If you do need public assistance, always have a goal in mind. Have an end-date in mind. It's important for your future and your child's future.

Borrowing

Try not to borrow from relatives and friends. Sometimes it can't be helped, but many friendships and families break-up over borrowed money. It's hard to pay back money that you borrow because it's hard to get ahead when you spend the money and then have new expenses. It's hard for the lender to collect from you, and that leads to resentment.

Education and Money

> *The sum of the square roots of any two sides of an isosceles triangle is equal to the square root of the remaining side. Oh joy! Rapture! I got a brain! How can I ever thank you enough?*
> *–The Scarecrow from the Wizard of Oz after being awarded a diploma from the Wizard.*

I sometimes felt like the Scarecrow because I never felt like I had any smarts until I got my degree. Then I need another and another. Was I any smarter after going to college? I think my brain and capacity for learning was probably the same whether I went to college or not. What I *did* learn was how to complete projects, how to do research, how to write, how to compete in an academic setting, how to read, how to learn, and how to feel more confident.

Sure, Bill Gates and several other successful business people never went to college, but they are exceptions to the rule. They had a vision and the confidence to pull it off.

Can you start a business without a degree? Sure, but you've got to know how to do it and have enough start-up money to do it.

My primary reason for believing that teen mothers need to complete at least high school and then go to college is to set an example for your children and to increase your life-time earning power. Side effects of getting an education are increased self-confidence, increased respect from society and other people, and increased value to society.

In 2012, economists estimate that college graduates will, over their lifetime, earn a million dollars more than high school graduates. Of course, if you've got student loan debt that has to be paid back, but a college degree increases not only your self-esteem, but your earning power.

So, if education is the key to higher earning power, how do you do it with a baby and little money? High school is free in this country if you go to public schools. You will be tired and it will be complicated, but you can and must finish high school in order to move on to the next phase of your life and to give your child a good example.

You might be tired, but you have your age on your side. You'll bounce back.

You can go to a community college and transfer to a state university for the last two years of your degree. College tuition isn't as expensive as you might think. Look into grants and student loans at the college nearest you. Find out if they have a day care facility.

Online schools are common now and many give four-year degrees. Some are expensive, so do your research. While you'll save on day care, you might find it hard to focus online with a baby to care for. The cost of the degree might be more than a community college would cost.

There are ways to get free tuition for college or trade school. When you look for a job, try to find one that has not only health insurance, but education benefits. One of my first jobs was at a university. I was envious of the students who went there on their parents' dime. Then I discovered that I got so many free credits every quarter as a benefit of my employment. During the two years I worked there, I amassed one year of college credit, and then it inspired me to finish my four-year degree.

One last thing about education: some young women believe that if they're still with their boyfriend, they don't need to finish their own education. Should you sacrifice your own education and support him through his? I say no. Hopefully you'll always be together. Hopefully he'll get a good job and support all of you. But what if you are not always together? What if you need two incomes? Something else happens when one partner sacrifices goals for the other person; resentments and jealousy sets in, feelings of inadequacy develop, and sometimes couples break up over it. When couples say that one partner changed and the other didn't, it usually means that one followed his or her goals and the other let them fall away.

Money Tips

- Don't be afraid to look at your financial situation. Many people, not just young people, give up on "looking" at their money. They're afraid of what they'll see; mounting debt, too little money, too little savings, too many bills, the possibility of losing your job, or even homelessness. Common mistakes: not looking at your checking account balance (if you have a checking account), not adding up every cent you're spending and figuring out where your money goes, and not counting what your parents and relatives contribute to your living expenses and baby expenses. Not knowing and not wanting to know leads to real trouble when you're out on your own and paying the majority of your own expenses. Knowing where you stand will lead you to good decisions about when to get a place of your own and how far away to move from your family.
- Reject debt. Pay off credit card balances. Credit cards are a good idea sometimes, but usually for emergencies. It's easy to buy "luxury" items such as clothing and makeup and use your credit card. Credit card debt tends to get away from you and grow and grow. That's because you are usually paying a high rate of interest on your credit card, and so if you buy something on "sale" you'll really be paying more for it.

- Accept as little financial help as possible from family and friends. Sometimes you will need help. But, if you pay for as many of your and your child's expenses yourself, you'll be better prepared to live on your own.
- Save money when you can. I remember what it's like to be young; you want to look nice so you spend money on clothing and beauty items. If you live at home and are living rent-free, try saving one-half of any money that you earn or is gifted to you. You'll need a saving cushion for emergencies.
- Use help when it's available. If you need food stamps, don't let pride stop you. If you need to get food from the food bank, don't think about it; just do it. Don't suffer in silence if it's caving in on you. Get child support (court ordered) is you can. It's not for you; it's for your child. Confide, don't hide.
- Remember to thank those who help you and to help others when you can. You don't have to reward them with money or gifts. Words are always appreciated. Trading babysitting or housework is always appreciated.
- Don't let help hinder you. Sometimes when people accept help such as food stamps, welfare, or gifts or loans from family, they become so dependent on the help that it prevents them from earning more or from accumulating wealth. For instance, it might be difficult to get food stamps if you own a house, but the goal should be to have a house, not to continue on food stamps.
- Have money goals. Have short-term and long-term realistic goals. For short-term, maybe you want to pay for college (community college is affordable and so in online schooling), or maybe you want to buy your own baby supplies. Long-term goals might be moving out of your parents' house, buying a car, or buy a house.
- Don't resort to "magical thinking." Most of us hope to win the lottery. I have always purchased lottery tickets. If you're counting on it, then it becomes magical thinking.
- Learn the difference between "need" and "want" whenever you have the urge to buy. Teenagers love the latest clothing and shoes and purses. Especially today when television and

advertising influences our lives so much. Buy what you need first, then what you need.
- Shop consignment stores, second-hand stores, and garage sales. You'll be surprised that many near-new or new-with-tags baby and adult clothing items can be snagged for very low prices. How about trading baby clothing with other young moms? There are also websites that allow you to do this.
- Have three months living expenses saved. This sounds hard, but if you get a windfall (a bonus from a job, a birthday gift, or a tax refund), but half of it away for a rainy day. It's hard when you want or need something, but it will save you some day.
- Remember the "latte factor." Cut the once-a-day coffee habit to once-a-week, maybe. What can you squeeze out of your budget? Do you get your nails done every week or every two weeks? Do you go to an expensive hair salon? You have to take care of yourself, but see what you're willing to sacrifice to save for your baby or for school.
- Remember, you will one day have all the money you need and more.
- Traffic tickets, parking tickets, and fines add up.
- Trade babysitting and day care with other trusted moms.
- Give back 10%. It doesn't have to be money—it can be time or babysitting or barter. Giving back makes you feel wealthier. I grew up in a farm family. We didn't have much money, but had an abundance of food and necessities. My mother always made a point to round up items to "give to the poor." I later realized that we could have been considered poor—but I never felt poor. Sometimes giving to others makes us feel good about ourselves and makes up realize how wealthy we really are.
- Don't do anything illegal for money. Ever. It might be tempting to sell drugs or be a "temporary prostitute" but the price could be more than any temporary gain. If someone offers you a job that seems "too good to be true," question the person and do your research.
- Don't get overwhelmed. No self-pity.
- What can you do to make more money and to get your income to rise?

So...

You deserve to have money. You deserve to have a good paying and rewarding career. You deserve to have a house and nice things. You deserve to have a good safe car. Some people believe that teen moms deserve to be poor and to stay poor. Americans also love a good "rags to riches" story. It's all up to you. It's hard, but you can choose your own story.

Your child deserves it. Say to yourself you deserve and your child deserves. All of us deserve to be in the 1% of wealthy people. You might as well shoot for it. Don't feel an obligation to keep yourself poor or to downplay success just because you are a young mom.

Tools for Your Journey

- **Goals:** Write down your money and career goals and share them with your family. Do you want to go to college? Is there one career you'd love to have? Have an action plan detailing how you will make this happen. Make a budget. Money is a huge issue for young parents. You and your family hadn't planned on this. A budget shouldn't overwhelm you, but it should give you guidelines. We'll talk about budgets later, but generally, a budget has a column for what you have coming in and a column for what you have going out. Everything should be included.
- **Dreams:** Don't give up on them, even if you have to change them a little. You want to be an artist? You can still work on your art while going to school and taking care of your baby. Carve out a few minutes each day to work on your dream.
- **Thank You:** Remember to thank those people who help you financially. Thank your parents for letting you live at home. Thank people who babysit for you or give you baby clothing.
- **Connection:** Take a finance class. Look for advice online.
- **Ask for Help:** Ask your family for help and tell them exactly what you need to make your goals happen.
- **Gratitude:** Be grateful for the things you have. Give back 10% if you can (if not money, then time or passed-on baby items).
- **Take Responsibility:** Write down your budget. Keep track of what you spend and how you spend it. Don't accumulate unnecessary debt.
- **Take Advantage of Time:** You are young. You may be living with parents, grandparents, or relatives. Use the time to get your education or training. You will probably be tired. You're young and you will recover.

nine

Help Soup

I'm sitting in a training room for my new job, my first real "career" job. It's the era of "new-age thinking" and the first of a stream of self-help books have become available. The trainer is giving us a time-out from our grueling schedule by having us listen to tapes by Dr. Wayne Dyer. He's known for books with clever titles, like <u>Pulling Your Own Strings</u>, and <u>You'll See It When You Believe It</u>. I hang onto every word. Dr. Dyer has a deep hypnotic voice and uses it as an instrument to persuade us that we can get over whatever obstacles are in our way, get over our fears and phobias, and become successful just as he has.

For the first time in a long while I feel hope for my future. I feel that I've climbed up a tall ladder to that place where several people told me that I'd have to climb to in order to get to "bottom."

Later, I bought every book he wrote and read them from cover to cover. I got a tidbit or two from each book, but that was enough to help me. Dr. Dyer told me *what* I should feel, but didn't really tell me *how* to get there. I would have to figure that out myself. Many self-help gurus followed his path, and I think some got better at telling people how to make things happen instead of giving us a jolt of inspiration that would fade two days after the class. Most of us like a good pep-talk, but we also need to know how to get out of a rut, how to find time to work on our goals, how to set goals, and how to feel better about ourselves without saying "I love you" into a mirror each morning.

You're lucky you have so much information out there to help you. You have almost *too* much. The Internet is filled with blogs and forums and online books and other downloadable material. It's also filled with opinions, inaccurate information, and sales pitches. You have the task of finding what helps you and what doesn't help. Everyone is different and so you have to find your own way. Information can guide you though. I caution you to be open to receive the advice and information you need, but to be wary of those that might take advantage of you. You shouldn't pay for help if you can't afford it. There are so many free resources that if you can't afford ongoing psychological help, you can find good and free or very inexpensive help. If you have big problems that you cannot tackle on your own (such as substance abuse), get the best help you can afford.

I remember taking my young daughter (she was five) to a psychiatrist because she had been acting up in school. After about five visits and many dollars, I asked him how many sessions he thought she would need. "Oh, she'll be with me until she's eighteen."

I called *bullshit* on it immediately. I admit that I didn't say it to him, but I never took her back. Nothing should take that long, and I believe it. It turned out that she had an undiagnosed hearing problem that caused her to have issues in school. There's no way this guy, who had several degrees from prestigious schools, would have helped her.

So, use your own judgment. You have good instincts as a mother. Use them. Use your common sense. Use advice from those you trust. Don't just turn your problems over to someone else and expect miracles. If you feel something isn't quite right about the advice you're given or about the person who gives it, follow your instincts. Following your instincts (not just what you desire, but what you feel is right) makes miracles happen during the parenting journey. The miracle happens along the way as you're raising your child. The miracle happens every day.

There are lots of advice books and advice television shows and advice experts out there. My condensed soup version for success: what goes around comes around; what you think about tends to happen; what you expect usually happens; how you treat other people is how they eventually treat you; you attract what you believe you deserve; and positive thinking attracts positive results.

It isn't magic, but it works. It might not work the way you think it will—not instantly and automatically. For instance, say you've been working hard and harder and harder and then years later you realize that you're out of debt and you've got savings and a good job with a good network. Your goal didn't happen magically and it didn't happen without setbacks and frustration along the way. If you give up on your goals, your goals give up on you.

How do you sort out all the advice and parenting methods and self-help strategies? It's good to read and research lots of them to "try them on" and decide what works for you. The way I approach things is to read about them. You don't have to buy a book or subscribe for help. There are forums and blogs and book excerpts and video and audio snips from real people. The problem is sorting this blast of information into something you can use. Much of the information contradicts other information.

Some of the advice may not apply to you. There are experts out there whom I admire and might help you. I read many self-help books as they came out, and at the time I got something from almost all of them. I recommend reading as many different books as you can and not taking any of them as gospel, but using those things that help you and tossing the rest. Some of the books I read early on that helped me were books by Dr. Wayne Dyer, Dr. Marianne Williamson, Oprah, and biographies of women who were in my situation. I also enjoyed reading inspirational books by people who had overcome diversity much greater than my own. You have to find what inspires you. What gets you fired up? What motivates you? What moves you?

My philosophy: If you are religious, then use your religion, if you consider yourself "spiritual" or believe that forces in the universe can guide you and work for you, then use that. Building a belief system and a healthy self-esteem takes some people a lifetime. Some people seem to be born with confidence and a healthy self-esteem in spite of horrible odds against them. Some people have resilience or ability to overcome adversity.

Be Fearless but Careful

It's good to take risks. If you have a goal that others seem to think is out of your reach (getting a college degree, becoming a doctor, etc.), have faith in yourself. It's good to do things you are afraid to do. It's good to do things that make you uncomfortable if they help you grow or achieve your goals. It's not always comfortable to go to college. It's not always safe and free of anxiety.

I watched a television show where a young man of twenty quit medical school in order to write a best-selling novel. He moved from a cushy situation where his rather wealthy parents were paying his medical school tuition and other expenses while allowing him to live rent-free in their home. His novel didn't take off as it might have hoped and he was left hanging. Had he done his research; that many first books and novels don't really make much money, the young man might had stayed in medical school and written his book on the side as did Michael Crichton, who wrote <u>Jurassic Park</u>.

Educated risks are ones where you do some research and get advice ahead of time before actually taking one choice over another. By now, you may be questioning your choice to raise your child. I know I did at various phases of raising my daughter. You may realize after your baby was here in the world and in your home, that you hadn't gotten all the information about how costly and tiring and what an awesome (as in BIG) responsibility it is to raise a child.

It's best not to question and regret a road we've taken, but to make that road the best road we can with the best destination. Forget about past choices (except for the brief periods they pop into your brain to remind you to make good future choices) and look to the future and get as much input and information as you can.

For instance, the young man who decided to throw away his medical school experience did so on advice from his friends. Those same friends had no direction themselves, it seemed, and maybe they were not the best people to give him advice.

Find Help

I repeat this mantra often throughout this book. Most people fail to seek help, because they never needed it before and they don't know how. Finding the right people for direction and advice is one of the most difficult parts of any decision-making process. Everyone has a different opinion and different motives. Maybe your friends really don't want you to go to college because it might undermine their own decision not to. Maybe your mother is afraid she'll get stuck babysitting too often and doesn't want you to waste your time going to school. Maybe your boyfriend is jealous or afraid you'll outgrow him if you get more educated.

Try to think of your child not as an extension of yourself, but as a separate being for whom you are ultimately responsible. Make each choice with your baby in mind. Make each choice thinking about the short-term and long-term consequences. Maybe you want to be a stay-at-home mom and going off to college isn't an option. Luckily today we have online schooling or night school. Think in terms that you have MORE options now, not fewer.

Be Careful and Wise in Love

Women are well-known for their love mistakes. Men make them too, but when children are involved women are sometimes more vulnerable to making mistakes with men. When we're in a vulnerable situation, we become targets sometimes to relationships that aren't healthy, that we can't get out of, or that are damaging to our children.

Try to rely on yourself first and then look for love. Most girls want love immediately. They want a "family" because they've already got the child and feel they need the completeness of a partner to make a family. It's important to feel loved, but please don't look for someone to "take care of you" until you can take care of yourself.

Make More Money

You may have to start at a low-paying job that you hate, but as soon as you are there, start thinking of ways to make more money. Can you do a better job than everyone else so that you get a raise? Praise? A promotion? Will a degree or training help? What job opportunities are in your area? What are your talents? What do you love to do? What can you create that will earn "mail box money." MBM (Mail Box Money) is what my husband calls income that just "rolls in" because of some product or service your created. Books are like that. You write a book once and it pays royalties many times. Records are like that. So are inventions and investments.

Don't risk your lively-hood over an idea, but if you've got them, don't be afraid to work on them. Don't be afraid to make more money.

Life's a Mystery

I believe in "synchronicity." Certain people or opportunities or things come across our paths at certain opportune times. It's our responsibility to reach out and grab at those opportunities while they are there. Sometimes it's hard to know why you have met a certain person or why you lost a job that you wanted. Sometimes it's because you need that person later or that you come across an even better job.

Use Each Day Wisely (and Take a Few Days Off)

I do believe in hard work. I'm the worst at wasting time. If I think I have a year to finish a project, then I'll take a year. If I think I have two years, then I will take two years. Lately I've come to realize that many things can be done much faster than I realized. I've watched MTV's Teen Mom show. Many times a young woman will take forever (as in years) to get her G.E.D. You can get a college degree in four years. I know it's hard with a baby. It's hard without a baby. It gets harder the older you get.

I saw a movie once where the guy said, "I'm too old to go to college. I'm forty years old."

The other character said, "How old will you be in five years?"

The guy says, "I'll be 45."

"Then you'll be 45 with a college degree. Otherwise you'll be 45 without a degree"

Remember to celebrate your successes, even if others seem lukewarm to them. I remember feeling that nothing I did (college, career, and marriage), ever trumped the fact that I was a teen mom. It was as if it was stamped on my forehead. You *got a degree? So what. You still had a baby at 17.*

Some people will never be on your side. That's okay. Not everybody will believe in you or support you. That's why you have to be your own cheerleader sometimes. Give yourself a reward. Or better yet, hang with people who appreciate your accomplishments. My husband is that for me and always has been. My grown children are a great support system for me. It might not be a husband or boyfriend who is completely in your corner. It might be a friend, a teacher or a mentor.

Don't Work Harder, Work Smarter

While working in the corporate world, I heard that bit of advice often. It's hard to grasp what it means, but I came to believe it means do whatever you can (legally and ethically) to get a better job that you truly enjoy. It's true that those at the top don't have to work as hard because they delegate to others. They've become successful enough (probably through hard work and smart decisions) that they don't have to do the really hard or somewhat demoralizing work anymore. While you're working any job, figure out how long you'd like to do that work or if it's the kind of work you want to do.

It's best not to quit a job until you have another. If the job is unbearable or abusive, then you have no choice. Always look ahead. How can you make more money? Will another degree help? Will a career change help? Is there a way to start your own business or monetize your own idea?

Figure out what you're good at. Write down what you do well and what you want to do well. Everybody had some talent. Doing this will help you decide how to direct your education or training. If you aren't sure, ask someone else what they think you're good at or what they think you'd be good at. Then, really think about it.

Be Grateful

I would tell that young me, if I could go back, not to expect help just because I was young, but to thank those who did help me. I'd tell her to be grateful for every bit of help, every bit of understanding.

Forgive

Before you go on a journey of revenge, dig two graves
—Confucius

I'd also tell that young me to forgive (and *forget* if possible) those people who didn't understand my situation or who made fun of me or who made my life and my daughter's life more difficult. I'd forgive because it only hurt me to carry any burden of hate or resentment or envy. Don't waste energy having a long-term "hate fest" with anyone, including a family member, a boyfriend, your child's father, or anyone else. Hating takes energy away from doing.

While I'm at it, I would ask for forgiveness for those that I forgot to thank and for those that I took advantage of.

Careful What You Say

Some of the most hurtful remarks in my memory are those that I overheard. It's heart wrenching to walk in while someone is saying really negative things and then you realize those things are about you. It's the most hurtful thing to overhear your mother or father or grandparent saying something bad about you.

Most of the time these remarks come from frustration or anger or they simply need to vent. How nice it would be if everyone would talk to you about those things that bug them instead of venting to others. This type of communication isn't really communication at all. It's called "triangulation." Triangulation is giving information to someone other than the person who needs to hear it. Sometimes the person is secretly hoping it will get back to you and that things will change. That way, they don't have to take any flak for saying it.

Let your child overhear you saying nice things about them.

Don't let him or her overhear or hear you saying negative or nasty things to them. You can say you're sorry later, but they never really forget. They take it to heart.

Help Each Other

Woody Allen once said that he wouldn't want to join a group that would want him as a member.

Sometimes teen moms don't want to identify with other teen moms. They want to identify with their former friends. But, there is something comforting and welcoming about a group of people who are in a similar situation.

You really are not alone. There are hundreds of thousands of teen mothers and adults who were once teen mothers. You can help each other. You can start a group or join a group. You can reach out so that you don't feel alone and they don't feel alone. Resist the urge to isolate yourself with your child. I've seen this many times and I've done it myself. You might find that as your friends drift away, the temptation is to become a "team" with your child. It's good to feel connected and protective of your child—you have to be—but you need other people too.

Things I Wish I'd Known

There is a trick that therapists sometimes use. They ask you to go back in time to the younger you and tell that person what you know now. Here is a list of what I would tell that young me:

- You are strong
- You are smart.
- You should follow through with your ideas, even if you have to throw them away sometimes.
- You learn from every failure. Each failure takes you a step forward to success. Edison once said that, "I am not discouraged, because every wrong attempt discarded is another step forward.
- You are right much of the time. When you are wrong, you will learn from it.
- You can accelerate your success when you fail faster.
- You should follow your instincts more often. Many times they are right and a few times they will save your life.
- Self-esteem comes from accomplishment, not from other people.
- You will become accomplished in many things; cooking, parenting, going to school, reading, writing, having a career, and many more things.

- Some of the men you will cry over just weren't right for you.
- *Most* of the men you cried over weren't right for you.
- You create memories for your children every day. Everything you do today might be remembered by your child. Do you want her to remember you this way? Do want her to have the burden of this memory?
- You can't take back a hurtful thing that you say to your child. You can't take back a slap or a shake. Kids remember the good things, the kind things, and the compliments as easily.
- You are responsible for making the best choice for your children and not just for yourself and what makes you feel good at the time.
- Nobody can make you feel bad about myself without your permission (borrowed from Eleanor Roosevelt).
- You don't have to tell everyone your life's story just because they ask.

My Last Bit of Advice

"The best revenge is massive success."
–Frank Sinatra

Prove them wrong. Many people say teen mothers cause crime and their children become criminals. I say it doesn't have to be that way. Statistics tell us that most teen mothers are high-school dropouts. I say all teen mothers should get a high school and then a college education. Statistics show that many teen mothers leave their children or have them taken away. I say it doesn't have to happen. Prove them wrong; the critics, the haters, the talking heads who have never met a teen mom, the "friends" who deserted you, the teachers and career counselors who don't believe in you. Get your education. Go as far as you think you can go, then go higher; aim your goals high. Rise above. Don't become a statistic; become successful and help your children become successful. Success is the best revenge. It's the only way I like to use the word revenge.

Prove them wrong.

End